Taking Charge of Your Career

CHANDOS
INFORMATION PROFESSIONAL SERIES

Series Editor: Ruth Rikowski
(email: Rikowskigr@aol.com)

Chandos' new series of books are aimed at the busy information professional. They have been specially commissioned to provide the reader with an authoritative view of current thinking. They are designed to provide easy-to-read and (most importantly) practical coverage of topics that are of interest to librarians and other information professionals. If you would like a full listing of current and forthcoming titles, please visit our web site www.chandospublishing.com or email info@chandospublishing.com or telephone +44 (0) 1223 891358.

New authors: we are always pleased to receive ideas for new titles; if you would like to write a book for Chandos, please contact Dr Glyn Jones on email gjones@chandospublishing.com or telephone number +44 (0) 1993 848726.

Bulk orders: some organisations buy a number of copies of our books. If you are interested in doing this, we would be pleased to discuss a discount. Please email info@chandospublishing.com or telephone +44 (0) 1223 891358.

Taking Charge of Your Career

A guide for library and information professionals

JOANNA PTOLOMEY

Chandos Publishing

Oxford · Cambridge · New Delhi

Chandos Publishing
TBAC Business Centre
Avenue 4
Station Lane
Witney
Oxford OX28 4BN
UK
Tel: +44 (0) 1993 848726
Email: info@chandospublishing.com
www.chandospublishing.com

Chandos Publishing is an imprint of Woodhead Publishing Limited

Woodhead Publishing Limited
Abington Hall
Granta Park
Great Abington
Cambridge CB21 6AH
UK
www.woodheadpublishing.com

First published in 2009

ISBN:
978 1 84334 465 0

British Library Cataloguing-in-Publication Data.
A catalogue record for this book is available from the British Library.

Typeset by Domex e-Data Pvt. Ltd.
Printed in the UK and USA.

Printed in the UK by 4edge Limited - www.4edge.co.uk

Contents

Preface and acknowledgements

Writing a book has never been a dream of mine and has mainly been the result of organic growth rather than design. My career – like this book – has been a marathon and a sprint at the same time, and perhaps a few more lines on my face especially in my 40th year. This book builds upon the ideas that I have accumulated and actioned over the last twenty years or so in my career. This career journey has been in the library and information industry (public, private and independent sector) and also via another industry sector where I trained and worked as a construction planning engineer.

This book has been written mainly to share my commitment and passion for the world of libraries and information services. I have been inspired to craft my career as an information professional and this book represents what I have learned and the tools I have utilised.

I would like to thank the many colleagues, clients and mentors I have worked with and for over my career. In some instances you gave your time, your interest, your words of wisdom and also when required the kick up the backside. There are too many people to list but you have all genuinely shaped the person I am today and are an important part of my ongoing journey. For my friends, colleagues and clients in the library and information world I only hope to give as much back.

This book would not have been possible without the practical and emotional support of my husband Eddie – you really are 'Eddie the wonder boy'! This book is dedicated to my husband Eddie, daughters Lara and Alice, sisters Frances and Patricia, dad George and to the memory of those who are not with us now.

Joanna Ptolomey

List of checklists

About the author

Joanna Ptolomey is a qualified librarian and works as an independent library and information professional. She has also worked as a librarian in the public sector in healthcare and in the private sector for a major worldwide consultancy. Her work portfolio covers research projects, consultancy, bespoke training courses and writing. The author is based in Glasgow, Scotland, in the UK.

The author may be contacted at:

E-mail: *info@joannaptolomey.co.uk*
Website: *http://www.joannaptolomey.co.uk*
http://www.facebook.com

Introduction

I am a qualified library and information professional working at the sharp end of the library and information services (LIS) sector on information management and delivery solutions for users. I am enthusiastic and truly passionate about the value of the LIS industry and the role the LIS professional can play for its users. To be absolutely honest, if I didn't believe that what we provide as professionals and the impact our services could have then I would find it incredibly difficult to get out of bed in the morning. I have experience and evidence of this having worked for over twelve years as a library and information professional in the public, private and independent sectors.

The LIS industry landscape is vast and finds its way into many industrial sectors while the core skills and competencies of the LIS professional open routes into many different types of information job. This is, of course, good news to have so many opportunities open and available to the LIS professional. However, it can make it quite a difficult career path to navigate. Where do you start? Where do you get experience? Is any LIS experience better than niche industry sector experience? In charting my own course through the industry I have heard many fellow professionals and colleagues also ask themselves key questions on what they should do and how do they decide and manage their career around and in the industry.

The key problem for most LIS professionals has been in finding a single source (or gateway) to pull out all the strands that are required for managing a LIS career. Like myself, they have used brilliant books, read wonderful articles, used the library and information professional association resources and accessed various tools to help manage their transition into the industry, their professional development and their moves upward in organisations and also across into different information sectors. Managing your career can be a time-consuming and complex task which is more of an issue if there is no structure. This book is designed to provide that structure and methodology for the LIS professional.

On my journey through the LIS sector I began to search for a central point of information for taking on board ownership, responsibility, methods and tools for LIS professionals taking charge of their career. Furthermore, this resource should not just be a signpost or a depository for information but should be a journey of enquiry for the information professional. It should act like an action research project; there should be enquiry, reflection, introspection, self-awareness and self-knowledge through to practice. The outcome of this search and journey is the book you are reading now. This book encapsulates a worldwide search to gather useful information, methodologies and tools to aid the LIS professional in taking charge of their career. The research has not been limited to the information sector; after all it would be quite self-righteous and pompous as an industry if we thought we had the best advice and solutions wrapped up only in our own industry.

I know that managing your career as an information professional can be partially managed by our LIS employers, but it is a two-way process. It would be rather childish to wait for our employer to tell us how we should chart our career and what skills we need and/or require. There is an element of responsibility for managing our careers and by taking on this responsibility we can make our relationship with our employer better.

I have enjoyed the variety of work available to the information professional and the diverse nature of where you can work. My practice as a LIS professional has always been about showing 'value' and tangible outcomes. This book follows the same principles for anyone who reads and participates in the book processes so that you, as a fellow LIS professional, will able to manage and steer your career to give you the most successful and tangible outcomes.

The information and library sector today is an exciting challenge for the professional, and there are opportunities available whether the economy is in full growth or even decline. There are career challenges at every corner, whether you want to stay in a particular sector or organisation, are looking to change sectors or move up the management ladder, or are entering the sector for the first time. Each of these moves can be difficult and complex to manage with the transformational changes sweeping our industry, but especially with the pace at which we seem to live our lives these days. This book gives the information professional the chance to reflect on and evaluate their career, and to manage it in a more systematic way.

This book is about enquiry rather than instruction and asks you how you want to shape your career as an information professional and what tools can help you to do so. Each chapter comes complete with reflection points where you will be called on to apply introspection and self-awareness to work out your true self-knowledge. I am well aware that this is not always an easy task and if you find these reflective points difficult by yourself, then invite a colleague on the journey with you or seek a mentor or coach. However, I would advise you not to be tempted to skip over the reflective sections – if you do so ultimately you will get less from the book.

This book is about rethinking your career in a refreshing and systematic way to take into account your professional and personal goals. The book is aimed at all levels of professionals within the LIS sector. It will serve as a guide for understanding the industry sector, auditing and understanding your career to date, discovering how and why you want to work and what practical tools and guidance can help you to move forward. This book should serve as a daily handbook on what makes you tick and how you can manage career shifts when you want to. It is particularly useful for people who have worked for a number of years and wish now to reassess their journey so far and are ready to make changes. Students at undergraduate and postgraduate levels will also find it particularly useful as a guide to starting and planning their career. However, this book is not about 'how to get a job' – it is much more than that.

At the heart of the book is a methodology called 'personal strategic planning'. This methodology allows the LIS professional to work out a baseline for what is important to them in a career and provides techniques and tools for moving forwards and realising your goals. I have written this book in an accessible style and straightforward manner from a practitioner's point of view. I am a 'jobbing librarian' and I understand the need for practical help and tips in managing careers in the LIS sector. As such the book readily discusses what to do when things go wrong and how to make you feel that you are in charge of your own career. In particular:

- it draws on the author's experience of moving between different LIS sectors having worked in the private and public sectors;

- it draws on the author's experience of successfully moving and adapting skills from a career in another industry sector;

- it provides a methodology and a set of workable tools for you to discover what you want from your career, outlines steps for moving forward and shows you how to reassess yourself on a regular basis.

This book has been designed to be environmentally friendly – it is not designed to be used once and then discarded. Its re-use value is high. The book does not seek to instruct you on what you need to take charge of your career and set you on that one and only path. You will find that constant monitoring of your needs is required to reflect your personal life, and this book can help you over a whole career.

Time and energy are such important commodities for this busy life we all seem to lead, so why waste it. Take the opportunity to spend some time in working out what you want from a LIS career, how to set goals and get tools to manage the change.

The book is structured into four main sections.

Part 1 The backbone – skip this at your peril

The chapters in this part form the backbone to taking charge of your career and are an essential part of the process:

- Chapter 2: Your LIS career I presume?
- Chapter 3: It's all about you
- Chapter 4: Check out the view – the LIS landscape

These chapters help you explore your personal preferences and experiences so far and ask you to identify the questions you have about your career.

Part 2 Everyday tools for taking charge of your career

These chapters provide a set of tools for the everyday management of your professional development and career. Do not underestimate the power that they will have and the tangible outcomes they can give:

- Chapter 5: Tips for keeping up with business as usual and managing change
- Chapter 6: Making the time for managing your career
- Chapter 7: Taking charge using project management as a tool

Part 3 Different stages of your career

This part covers specific periods in your career. The chapters are designed to be complemented by Part 1 and Part 2:

- Chapter 8: Career breaks
- Chapter 9: Starting out, making it count
- Chapter 10: Managing and leading
- Chapter 11: Going it alone – being an independent information professional

Part 4 A complete framework for personal strategic planning

This part brings all the other chapters together and shows how they can work. I suggest you don't skip straight to this chapter without having worked through at least Parts 1 and 2. I promise the results will be greater if you don't look for short cuts:

- Chapter 12: Personal strategic planning

This book aims to be practical and insightful in allowing you to reflect on and enquire about how an LIS professional can manage their career. Some of the chapters include subjects that have been addressed in other books but I believe they have never all been presented in one complete volume.

Are you ready to get to grips with you career as a library and information professional? Are you ready to see positive tangible results from your efforts? Are you ready to have more time and energy for focused and effective development of your career as an information professional? Do you want to know how to get the enthusiasm and momentum to direct your career? Then read on, and good luck.

Part 1

The backbone – skip this at your peril

Your LIS career I presume?

After you have read this chapter you will be able to:

- accurately define the particular questions that you have about your own career in the LIS sector;
- identify the issues that can cause the information professional not to take charge of their career;
- identify your career objectives and outcomes using verbs or action words.

Introduction

I realised quite early on in my career in the library and information sector (LIS) that sustaining and managing enthusiasm for and controlling the direction of my career could be difficult on a day-to-day basis. This included not just issues over career development, but also knowing how to handle and take advantage of useful opportunities and experiences that might arise, how to manage the questions I had and how to identify what direction I ought to take and the actions that would be required.

First of all, the LIS sector is a vast industry covering opportunities in the public, private and voluntary sectors. How can you tell which sectors may be a good fit for your interests, skills and ethics? What do we mean by public, private and voluntary sectors, and what type of opportunities are there for the LIS professional? Secondly, the sheer variety of work that is available for the LIS professional to do is enormous and ranges across the traditional, non-traditional, hybrid and independent fields. This may give you an idea of the size of the industry and, irrespective of your level and experience within the industry, you may be asking yourself 'where do I start and how do I know where to focus my energies?' For example, you are a new graduate entering the profession and focused on getting paid professional work, but with a huge industry open to you where do you start? This can also be a difficult situation for the 'not so new LIS graduate'. What do you do if you find yourself working as a clinical librarian but your interests lie in the media sector? How can you capitalise and build on your skills base in order to move into different sectors?

Apart from the broad range of jobs available there are other reasons that can contribute to the lack of success in managing your career. There is the question of time, and your ability – or lack of it – to manage it, depending on your point of view. The question of 'how do you sustain momentum and direction' in order to reach your desired goals is also a common enquiry. I have a normal life with the same professional and personal demands, wishes, expectations and responsibilities as most of you. Eating, drinking, sleeping, caring, relaxing, socialising, feeding and loving are some of the other things that we all do as well as working for money. We need money to live, but what is life without the things we truly care about? So with this in mind I have set about finding a method that will bring all the parts of our lives together, as LIS professionals and as private individuals, and make managing our careers an easier and more effective task.

I came into the LIS sector later on in life – for ten years or so before that I had been involved in some way or another with the construction industry. Those seemed like ten long years – have you ever spent time in the wrong job or career and watched time drag? Twelve years ago I started my career in the library and information world. These have been the twelve shortest years – have you ever noticed how time seems to swoosh along when you are in the right job or career?

It's a serious business this working thing. Not just from a financial point of view, which is important to all of us as we all need a certain amount of money to survive, but in the way it has power over our lives and can affect how we feel about ourselves in quite a deep and profound way. I know of academic librarians who ponder the issues of the hybrid librarian role, media librarians who question the role of folksonomies, and clinical librarians who struggle to incorporate Web 2.0 tools into their service in the light of their health trust's IT restrictions. I know many LIS professionals working across a spectrum of jobs who have all spent amazing amounts of time and energy discussing their careers as professionals, what their jobs are and how they feel about them. I have also met a few LIS professionals who insist that they don't care about their careers; they are only in it for the money. This is an argument I understand if you work in the City and your bonus (never mind your salary) is calculated in millions. I have never seen or heard of a LIS professional quote their salary in millions of pounds or dollars as yet. So, even if you feel that you just need a job to pay the bills, why not do something that you enjoy, as we all spend a substantial part of our lives working?

In my career as a LIS professional I have had high points and low points professionally and personally. There have been paid periods of work and unpaid periods of work, employment periods and unemployment periods and public sector and private sector working, and now there is independent working. Some of my career choices have been

13

unintentional through opportunities presenting themselves and others have arisen through strategy. However, the overriding effect is that I have (and I hope to continue) a successful career. In using the word success I use my own personal definition. Firstly, success, for me, is not driven by money; I need to earn a living to pay bills but I am not driven to make a fortune. Secondly, my personal life is a major factor to my happiness. Thirdly, useful and fulfilling work in an area in which I feel I can make a difference and is for the common good is also important. If I feel that in the work I do I can hit those targets then I am successful.

As a LIS professional have you ever asked yourself: 'Who is the most important person who has had the greatest impact on my career?' I hope you would say 'yourself', or this book will be really hard work for you. I think we all know that responsibility is key to taking charge of your own career. It is down to the individual to take the opportunity to learn new skills and take advantage of chances as they present themselves. Perhaps as you start out on your career – or indeed look back on what you have already achieved in your career – you never envisioned some ideas such as information literacy skills training for young adults, running critical appraisal sessions for a nurse-led clinic on smoking cessation, project managing the refurbishment of a library or measuring the impact of a literature search service.

Our lives today are complicated and it can indeed be a difficult challenge to separate what is work from what is your personal life. The intention of this book is not to debate or discuss work versus leisure, the distinctions between them and the reasons behind identity and work. These are questions for other books and other experts, though I have provided some further information at the end of the chapter. However, there does seem to be evidence to suggest that the way in which and pace at which we live our lives today and the importance of the function of what we do suggests that the boundaries to the idea of work and life being separate entities are becoming blurred. This can make it difficult to manage our careers. What if we have great intentions but find it hard to focus and keep the momentum going? As LIS professionals our lives are made up of work and personal stuff, so how do we reconcile these two parts of our existence? This book is not about how to get a job as a LIS professional, how to climb the LIS career ladder or how there is always a better LIS job out there – it is much, much more than that. This book sets out a methodology for embracing all that we hold dear and important to us, whether they be professional or personal issues, and working out how to bring them together.

The questions we have in mind

Irrespective of whether you are a new LIS graduate and looking for that first (or any) job, a professional with a few years' LIS experience who wants to use their skills in, say, the public library sector to specialise in a community health information programme or an experienced academic librarian looking to move into a leadership role, we all have questions about how we can manage this change process. Some of the questions are LIS-specific, but some are of a more personal nature. Here are some examples for you to ponder.

- Moving upwards in your career:
  - I am a public librarian with five years' experience and I want to move into a job with more responsibility. How do I make myself ready to show that I can do it?

- After more than ten years in the LIS industry I am unsure where to go from here. How do I audit my career and identify my next move?

- Having career breaks:

  - I am on a career break and want to plan to return to work part-time.

  - I have been having a career break for a few years. I am ready to return but have lost confidence in my skills and where I should place myself in the industry. How do I get back into work?

- Changing sectors:

  - I worked in a private sector business library. How do I re-use my competencies and build on my transferable skills?

  - I feel bored in my current LIS job and organisation. Do I need to change my job or my attitude?

- Time and project management:

  - My development consists of other people's ideas of what I need to do and how it fits in with the company's strategic plan. How can I take control of my own future, especially where I want to utilise my creative thinking processes?

  - Each year I set myself goals to increase my professional competences and profile – I never follow through. Where am I going wrong and how do I sustain momentum?

  - I feel so stressed by the volume of work, meetings and personal commitments that I cannot concentrate on making time for personal development. How can I make it all work better?

  - I have no sense of achievement at the end of the day and I am firefighting most of the time. What small changes can I make that will show real achievement?

- Understanding yourself:
  - I am in the wrong job. What do I do?
  - Do I have job burnout or job boredom?
  - How do I get more of a work–life balance?
  - I have shoehorned myself into jobs and now feel boxed into a particular LIS sector. What can I do?
- Starting out:
  - I am at library school. Where should I focus my job-hunting?
  - This LIS job is part-time, low-paid, not in an industry sector I had considered working in and lasts eight weeks – should I do it?
  - Should I do voluntary non-paid work?

Some of the examples above actually do relate to situations I have found myself in at some points in my career, but the others are so general in nature that most LIS professionals will have asked themselves these questions at some point. In fact, I am betting that a good proportion of you reading this book will have also asked yourself certainly some (or variations) of these questions. From my own experience as a LIS professional I have learned from these situations, and isn't hindsight a wonderful thing? I have also learned that the LIS sector is a very forgiving industry in which to work. There are numerous opportunities to adapt existing skills and learn new skills. Like most of you reading this book my personal situation has changed (as a result of either planned or unexpected events and opportunities) over the years and I have had to adapt. I have learned to become more confident in exploring ways and methods to get my personal and private life to be more complimentary and reach for that ever-elusive work–life balance.

How goes your LIS world?

I believe that most of you working out in the LIS sector would agree that taking a more planned and methodological approach to our careers could have a highly beneficial effect on us as individuals and professionals. However, as people we do not always approach such matters in a methodological fashion. We generally let things 'sail along', experiencing the not so highs and not so lows of what our life and careers can throw at us. We know that we could be 'doing more' to help ourselves in our careers, but it is usually a 'bombshell' that sparks us into life (or panic).

All of a sudden you are aware that things are not as great or as easy as they could be. You may recognise some or all of these experiences: the change in direction of a library service such as the convergence of IT with library management skills, a crisis in the financial markets with library services being the first to feel the effects of organisational cutbacks, that first professional post seeming a million miles away, a sudden death or illness in the family refocusing your attitudes, having family responsibilities which require a different style of working, a difficult work colleague, redundancy, or the stagnation of being too long in one particular LIS sector where you notice the same issues are still unresolved. As a LIS professional you also begin to experience something more subtle, but still quite unnerving when it happens. For example, you may find that your job has mutated into something unrecognisable and you now have responsibility for not just one library service, but a learning centre and an IT team. You wake up one morning and are completely bored by what you do, the delights of macroeconomic data no longer set your house on fire and you realise that you no longer care about the quality of your work and feel professionally isolated. Panic can set in rapidly and it is quite easy to lose your confidence. Each LIS professional's view will be different as their sector experience comes with its own set of issues and obviously we all have our own personal prevailing circumstances.

Let's not get too gloom and doom, but even a really positive experience can be difficult to manage. Consider the following examples of positive events.

- You may feel that you are ready to move up the career ladder into leadership and management. You have excellent operational experience in an NHS library, a business information service and the voluntary sector. You have a flair for creative problem-solving and want to move into a completely different LIS sector, but how do you approach it?

- You have been touted as an excellent candidate for a very senior position in your library service. The financial rewards are good, but deep down you know that it does not play to your best skills, coupled with the fact that it will take you into an area you have very little interest in. Should you shoehorn yourself or is there any other way you could manage the change and negotiate the structure of the position?

- You have just qualified as a LIS professional and you are excited by the prospects of putting all that theory into practice. But where do you start managing your career when your main concern is paying the bills and putting food on the table?

We have all experienced positive or negative situations as a LIS professional that can cause upset, disharmony and confusion. However, they are what they are – moments in time to be lived through and endured. The most important point is that there is no need to make this your life. Unfortunately most of us generally wait to experience the 'career crisis' in order to wake up and take note.

In all situations, whether positive or negative, there are opportunities for you to discover where you are and what you want, and to consider how to bring about the kind of change you are looking for. In case a few of you missed that last sentence, I did say opportunities. Accept that change happens and no matter what the situation you are in now it is possible to modify the outcome or change the status quo. It's time to manage that change, take charge of the situation and move on with your goals.

Why this book can help you

This is a book full of verbs – you know, the 'doing or action word'. You will find the use of verbs scattered liberally throughout. The remit of this book is to find what 'your verbs' will be, what questions you have formulated, what objectives you have discovered for yourself and what objectives you have set. Once you understand this, then you are ready to find out more about your skills, what the industry has to offer and the tools for managing the change.

This book sets out a methodology for taking charge of your career in the LIS sector. It takes account of the fact that the LIS industry itself is large and offers a wide variety of jobs whatever your skills, experience, interests and goals. It does not matter whether you are starting out on your career or are already established in the LIS sector, this book can help you. There are tips and ideas for getting to know who you really are, what is important to you and your life, and what tools you can use to help you move forward with your goals. It also considers what employment the LIS sector can offer you, the importance of researching your job market, how to create plans and strategies to reach your goals, how to keep the momentum going, how to unlock your creativity and how to monitor your career progress.

Essentially there are a few main themes within this book:

- working out where you are at the moment with your LIS career;

- working out what you want from your personal and professional LIS life;

- what type of work could be open to you in the LIS sector;

- what tools and coaching you can embrace to get you where you want to go as a LIS professional.

Reflection and understanding for this chapter

Using Checklist 2.1 (which you may copy as many times as you need) list your career questions, including verbs to set some objectives. For example, a few years ago my list read as follows:

How can I ...

- have two articles published?
- speak at a major conference?
- get experience in working on a committee?
- win a consultancy project?
- get training on Web 2.0 tools?
- have a better understanding of the LIS sector and its component parts?

Checklist 2.1 The questions you have in mind

In this space list your career questions, including verbs to set some objectives.

Further reading

Fincham, B. (2008) 'Balance is everything: bicycle messengers work and leisure', *Sociology*, 42(4): 618–34.

Gambles, R., Lewis, S. and Rappaport, R. (2006) *The Myth of the Work–Life Balance*. Chichester: Wiley Blackwell.

It's all about you

After you have read this chapter you will be able to use the three-stage plan to:

- state accurately what is important to you personally and as a LIS professionally;
- write your own LIS personal constitution;
- reflect on the career journey you have had up to this point;
- reflect on what you are good at and what makes you brilliant;
- consider the need for 'sounding boards' and mentors;
- understand why things didn't always work out well and put 'disappointments to bed'.

Introduction

This chapter is well and truly based in the practice of reflection, a process that leads self-awareness and ultimately to self-knowledge. The last two chapters should have convinced you that you and you alone are the linchpin in managing your career as a LIS professional. However, you will not be able to meet your requirements if you do not understand more about yourself and what is important to you. This chapter is dedicated to a better understanding of yourself as a LIS professional. You will be asked to reflect to encourage self-awareness and develop self-knowledge. In some ways this is at the heart of the book – it will say more about you than anything else. It is imperative that this chapter should be read and the checklists completed before you tackle any other in the book.

It is so easy to say that we are the most important people in our own careers, but how many of us actually believe that we are the masters of our own destinies? So often we can feel like flotsam and jetsam bobbing about on the different oceans of our lives, only managing aspects of our personal and professional lives when the need arises, such as when a crisis erupts or when we are compelled to address a situation that has got out of control. I think that most of us would love to start taking more of a proactive approach to our careers but it can seem like an overwhelming task.

Suggestions have been reported in the LIS press over the last few years of the impending doom within the industry and the demise of the LIS professional as we know it. We could dwell on this point, but personally I just don't believe it. I believe that the changes in the LIS industry have in fact had the opposite effect. It has opened up the LIS professional to a more challenging and rewarding industry, with even more opportunities to show that information management is still at the heart of many of the changes. These changes may have been engineered or organically developed, but at their heart they are just changes. Let me assure you that I don't live in a bubble and I am aware of the problems that many LIS sectors are facing, but I am asking that you view them in a different manner. Now we can either fear change or reconfigure our mindset to think about it differently, for example as an opportunity to enhance our lives in some way. It is sometimes our attitude to change that causes fear to set in.

This book does not set about to change your personal characteristics, but it does ask you to reflect on your attitude to change and the opportunities that almost always arise from such a situation. So with this more optimistic frame of mind I believe that the changes in the industry have opened up more opportunities for LIS professionals. For further information see Chapter 4 where I will consider more about how the LIS industry landscape has changed over the last decade and the exciting opportunities that as a result are now open to the LIS professional.

Let's start at the beginning before we think about moving forward. It is imperative that we understand where we are as people in the grand scheme of things. Quite simply, we need to understand what is important to us personally and professionally, and then audit, reflect on and then acknowledge our assets. We also need to understand what external factors and issues could be pulling at our ability to take charge of our careers and the choices we make.

Stage 1: Your personal constitution

What is important to you – a.k.a. your 'personal constitution'

We tend to live our lives as two separate entities – we have a work life and we have a personal life and never the twain shall meet. But it is almost impossible to live like this. Just ask yourself this: when things are going badly at work how does that affect your personal life? Are you irritable, tired, fed up generally, lethargic, annoyed? Can you be a complete pain in the 'you know what' to live or work with?

Do you feel that your work life does not match up to how you really want to live your life and wonder whether is it possible to use your own personal ideals to mould and affect your work life? This is what I call a 'personal constitution' and, believe it or not, we all have our own – you just may not be aware of it. A 'personal constitution' reaches into the bare bones of who we are as people, and getting to know your own constitution is possibly one of the most important and powerful things you can do for yourself personally and professionally. All organisations have (or should have) a constitution, it is their essence of being and without it they cannot describe how, why or what they do and the impact they hope to have. Quite simply a personal constitution is what makes you tick. Why do you want to be a library and information professional? How do you want to spend your life? How much time do you want to spend working? What interests do you have, including LIS sectors and skills sets? Where do you want to spend your time? Do you have dependents and how do you allocate more time to them? How important is money to you? What value do you place on leisure time? When you consider some of these areas then you are starting to understand your personal constitution.

So far so good. This all seems quite straightforward, but there is a catch. You have to be completely honest with yourself. I believe that I don't have an inbuilt mechanism to lie to other people, but what I have discovered over the years is that I have lied to myself constantly over decisions and issues while working as a LIS professional. I believe that I am not alone in behaving this way. We may think twice about lying to other people, but I believe that we easily lie to ourselves about these fundamental questions in our lives. How often do we 'brush things under the carpet', quietly thinking we will deal with them later?

Your personal constitution will be unique to you and I have developed a tool (Checklist 3.1) to help you discover more about *why* this is important to you and specifically *what* is important to you. The checklist may be copied and used as many times as you wish, but read through the next section on 'factors that affect your personal constitution' before attempting it.

Checklist 3.1 Working out your own personal constitution

Money

Go through the following questions:

- Is there a certain level of salary you would expect to earn?
- Is there a certain amount of money you need per month to pay the bills and live?
- Have you considered downshifting your lifestyle?
- Do you need further benefits like pension cover and health insurance?

Job sectors

Go through the following questions:

- Are you attracted to particular LIS sectors? If so, which?
- Do you prefer to work in a traditional library set-up?
- Do you prefer the private or the public sector?
- Do you want to work with the public?
- Would you like to work in a large or small organisation?
- Would you consider solo working?
- Would you consider independent working?

Personal considerations

Go through the following questions:

- Can you work full-time?
- Do you want to work full-time or part-time?
- Can you work weekends or evenings?
- Do you need flexible working?
- Do you like to work in a team or on your own?

(Cont'd)

Personal attributes

Go through the following questions:

- Do you enjoy repetitive operational type work?
- Do you enjoy project work?
- Do you have a short attention span?
- Are you a details person?
- Do you like a broad-brush approach?
- Are you focused on your job or is personal consideration just as important?

Factors that affect your personal constitution

Financial

We are all required to pay our way in life, unless you happen to have a trust fund, and I am guessing that not many of you fall into that bracket. Most of us starting out in the LIS sector will have been at university for a number of years either as an undergraduate or a postgraduate (perhaps four or five years), building up debt as well as life experience. The number one priority on graduating is therefore to get a job and earn money as quickly as possible. Not exactly a no-brainer, but does money continue to be your main driver?

My career had firstly taken me into the construction industry. I have a first degree in construction management and had worked as a planning engineer for a number of years. Therefore my entry into the LIS sector was a switch in career, and I had gone back to university for postgraduate studies putting my partner's and my own life into downshift mode. When people talk of downshifting today it is seen in terms of having a more fuel-efficient car, taking up yoga or eating organic food, and you will get no argument from me that these are very worthy endeavours. But it is hardly financial downshifting. What does it look like in practical terms? Perhaps not having a television and shopping from cut-price stores for food and clothes. New furniture to you is stuff other people take to the dump, camping is the new holiday activity, and knowing a dozen recipes that involve tins of tomatoes, pasta, lentils and cheddar cheese means you don't need the number for the takeaway.

Here are some other financial things that you may need to think about. Are you are willing to trade money for other things? Lifestyle may be very important to you – being able to buy clothes from whatever store you want, drive a good car, live in a certain neighbourhood and always have an exotic exciting holiday. However, there are always tradeoffs when maintaining a lifestyle. You may have to work harder for longer and incur more worry that your situation will change. You may have to spend less time with your family or friends. Salaries can vary quite a lot depending on the LIS sector you work in, so this could stop you from moving on to something else. For example, I reduced my salary when I moved from the private sector back into the health sector.

Money was more important to me when I started out but is less important now. However, I just found out today that my car needs more than just some screen wash and a new tyre after its winter service. I suppose the family room can wait for a set of curtains ...

Why do you work in the LIS sector?

It would seem important that because we spend a large proportion of our lives working, then it should be by doing something we find interesting or are naturally good at. I hear from library and information graduate course leaders that many aspiring LIS professionals are interested in working in the glossy media sector. What is it that draws you to a particular sector – a lifestyle or an image of what that sector says about you? Do some research and find out what a job in that LIS sector would actually entail. Perhaps you are interested in using specific skills such as those of a research analyst – what sectors could such skills be used in? In a technology-driven world, it could be IT and information management together with a niche area such as health that could lead to a specialism such as health informatics.

Is there LIS work that makes you want to get out of bed?

This is an important section and if you are starting out in the industry or looking to make changes and are unsure of what you would like to do then look at Chapters 4 and 9 for more advice. You may find that you are driven by your ethics to work only for a specific sector of the industry such as the public or voluntary sector, or perhaps for a specific user group such as the learning disabled, the terminally ill or disadvantaged young adults. Ask yourself some questions like: 'Do I want to make a difference to someone's life?' 'Is my real love in life music and film?' or 'Do I love the thrill of the business and financial sector?' Consider also whether you want to have contact with the public (such as a public, health or academic setting) or are you happy working within a closed organisation such as a financial or consulting institution? One of the main reasons I left the private sector was because some of the clients were at odds with my ethics and I worked in a very closed environment with little people contact. I returned to the health sector to continue making a contribution to the health of the population and enjoyed lots of people contact.

The most important reason for working in a particular sector is, I believe, that you enjoy the subject area. The excellent news is that library and information work is one of the broadest job groups for touching many industry sectors so you are bound to find something that 'floats your boat'. Chapter 4 will provide more information.

Personal situation

Firstly, do you have or want a personal life? That may seem like a strange question but there are some for whom work life and personal life are one and the same. Ultimately it is up to you how you choose to spend your life, so take a close look at what you absolutely want. If you have a personal life then probably high on your list is spending time with family and friends and socialising, holidays and perhaps volunteering.

Your personal situation will also influence your work situation, sometimes in a heart-stopping and serious way. Perhaps you have children or help care for a family member. Perhaps illness, relationships and the death of a family member have also touched you.

What format of work do you want?

The LIS sector opens up a variety of different ways to work, although some are more common to find than others. Questions like do I want to work part-time, full-time or flexible time, as an employee, solo worker or independent? Other things to consider are: 'Do I like doing project type work or do I prefer concentrating on operational LIS service work?'

Consider your personal attributes

There is no wrong or right answer to this, but it will give you an indication of how you as a person have natural tendencies and characteristics. Consider questions like: 'Do you have a short attention span?' 'Do you like detailed work with little interruption?' 'Do you like working in teams?' Most of us will have heard about personality types and the theories of American psychologist Katherine Briggs. She went on to develop the questionnaire called the Myers-Briggs Type Indicator that proposed a number of different ways that people prefer to work. There have also been many variations of this type of personality test over the years, and this book will not replicate that work. If you want to know more about this type of testing and find out more about how you work then there is a list of further reading at the end of the chapter.

My personal constitution – my example using Checklist 3.1

Hopefully this section of the chapter has set your mind thinking. Now let's put it down on paper. To help you get started with the thinking process for your own personal constitution here is my own. This list of bullet points provides the foundation for my personal situation. It also sets out the trade-offs I need to make in order to keep to my ideals. In brackets you will find the sections from Checklist 3.1 that I had considered.

- I work part-time and flexibly to get the most from my family life with two small children and a partner.

  Trade-off: I generally have to work parts of the weekend and some evenings (money, personal considerations, personal attributes).

- I need a certain amount of money to pay the bills, but time is a more important commodity to me.

Trade-off: Money is not always available for 'going out' and holidays can be more of the camping variety rather than exotic (money, personal considerations).

- I choose to have a specialism in the health-related sector because I believe in equality and accessibility to good healthcare for all, but use my generic information skills in other sectors.

Trade-off: In the UK working in the National Health Service (NHS) as a Clinical Librarian does not command the best salary, and now, as an independent worker, project availability can be severely affected by NHS budget constraints (job sectors, money, personal attributes).

- I believe that through the work I do I can actually make a difference to the health of the man in the street (albeit by an indirect and sometimes circuitous route).

Trade-off: Not all work can have high satisfaction standards (job sectors).

- I enjoy work and I like it to be challenging with variety.

Trade-off: I generally feel that each project has a steep learning curve for my body of knowledge (job sectors, personal attributes).

- I enjoy project type work.

Trade-off: This is not always possible and sometimes with a limited market I have to take on any work I can get (personal attributes, personal considerations).

- I know I have a short attention span and get bored easily.

Trade-off: I struggled with this attribute for a long time and found regular operational type jobs unrewarding (personal attributes, personal considerations, job sectors).

- I like my work to have tangible outcomes that have immediate uses and benefits.

  Trade-off: An ideal, but not always possible, I know (personal considerations, job sectors).

When you make up your own personal constitution it's very possible that you cannot tick all the boxes all the time – unfortunately not everything is possible. As you can see with my personal constitution, for everything that is important for me there is a trade-off. You will find the same. But these ideas are the 'holding down bolts' for you as a person. You will find that every few years you will need to reassess your personal constitution. As I work independently I generally reassess my situation on a yearly basis as it has changed remarkably over the last few years. For example, six years ago I had no children and a smaller house. In those six years I have had two periods of no work when I was pregnant and my children were under one. I have moved house to take account of my growing family unit and school availability. I now run a second car. I have to take into account school and kindergarten drop-offs and pick-ups. I have after-school activities. I enjoy keeping fit. I started writing for publication. There have been a couple of serious family health situations. I could go on ...

Stage 1: Reflection

- With reference to what you have read and my own personal example now use Checklist 3.1 to work out your own personal constitution.
- You can copy and re-use the checklist as many times as you need.

Stage 2: Reflecting on what makes you brilliant

This section is designed for you to reflect on yourself as a person and is about valuing your assets and skills. Let's ask ourselves a couple of very important questions: Do we value our assets? Is it modesty or ignorance that stops us from talking about ourselves as LIS professionals? I was born and raised in and around Glasgow, Scotland. Here in the UK we are generally modest about what we are good at and it has only been in the last five years that I have been able to specify and value my assets. For example, since I could remember I was always very good at organisation and planning, a talent that would later be called project management. For a long time I believed that most people were equally interested and good at using this tool. Obviously later (much later) I learned this was not true.

Conversely, I believe that we are generally quite good at spotting the best in others. Imagine you are talking to a LIS friend/colleague who is unsure about their ability to develop a new aspect of the public library for people with learning disabilities. They are thinking of moving on as they feel unsure of what they have to offer. What do you do? Generally most of us launch straight into the reasons why our colleague could fit this role, what skills they bring to a new team, why many colleagues value their counsel and creative thinking on hard-to-reach users, that they work hard to engender team spirit, that they have high standards in everything they do, etc. So why do we find it hard to do this for ourselves? It follows that if we find it hard to really understand or appreciate what we are good at, is it any wonder that we have no idea how to use this information to our advantage and make the right career moves for ourselves?

We take it for granted that if we are good at something then others are equally good at it. But think through some of the things you are involved in either with regard to LIS work (and also importantly non-LIS work) or pleasure. Think about the following questions as an aid to work out your skills.

- What is your part in a group – the organiser, the worker, the planner, the leader, the ideas person, the finisher, the details person? I am an ideas person, but definitely not a details person.

- What would the balance of the group be if you were not there? Creative, outspoken ideas people are great, but who would study the details and finish the project?

- What are your best qualities that you value? Perhaps you are considerate to others' needs, you are organised, you are energetic in your enthusiasm, you have a positive outlook even in bleak situations, you are level-headed, etc.

- What do other people value in you?

- Do you currently use your best qualities in LIS work? Perhaps you have advocacy skills that you use in volunteering work – how might they be used in your job?

- What would you like to achieve with your talents? Are you making full use of them in your current position or could they be exported elsewhere?

I understand that this section calls for more introspection and reflection than some LIS professionals may be comfortable with. If you are finding it difficult to work through this stage then perhaps team up with another LIS colleague, perhaps in a different job or organisation, and do the checklists together. If you are feeling braver then try and find a mentor. Just try and get started, so go on – throw modesty out of the window.

A sounding board or 'sounding off' board?

There is quite a lot we can do for and find out about ourselves as LIS professionals. But exploring on your own can sometimes be a difficult thing. Friends and work colleagues can be of great assistance and comfort, but sometimes we need just a little bit more. We need a much wider perspective of our situation and the industry in which we work. And if you are a solo worker like myself, then I believe that it is very important that you have people who you can turn to for advice. As people we can find it difficult to face up to certain aspects of our careers, the decisions (good or bad) we have made, what we are good at, what our blind spots are and how we have managed so far. All this is good work, but where do we go next? How do we put it all in context? How do we get a broader view of a situation and view it from a different angle? Most of us need a sounding board.

Perhaps most of you consider that you already have a sounding board to discuss the issues of the day, what makes you happy and what upsets you. Perhaps what most of us probably have is a 'sounding off board', that is a group of friends or colleagues who can help us get things off our chest, release the pressure a little, and sometimes that is all we need. We need to vent some anger, frustration, unhappiness, indecision and helplessness at someone. The problem with this method is that usually there is no strategy to move further beyond this. A point also to consider is that if we want to keep our friends and colleagues we cannot just 'offload' all our problems or issues onto them on a regular basis. Consider also, they are friends and colleagues so are they really going to tell you the absolute truth or make you think about things in a different way? They could be too close to you or the issues themselves.

The idea of mentoring has been around for a long time and was generally considered to be about the relationship

39

between the experienced craftsman and the apprentice. Nowadays there is a broader definition: the idea of skills, knowledge and wisdom being passed on. That seems like a brilliant idea. However, a word of caution. I learned to play the flute nearly thirty years ago and have had many teachers and mentors along the way. They gave advice on technique, creative style and taking my career as a flautist forward but I still had to do the practice and play the instrument. Having a mentor is not an excuse for someone else to take on the responsibility. You must be prepared to take what you learn from the situation and your mentor and apply it. You must be prepared to do the practice and homework, and don't turn up expecting a mentor to give you all the answers. Part of the fun (yes, I did say fun) is doing it yourself and finding yourself doing things that you never thought you would. For the record I didn't become a professional musician, but I still find time to play the flute.

Mentoring can be a formal or an informal process. Formal mentoring relationships are often run through professional associations, academic courses and workplace professional development plans. There are usually stringent guidelines and procedures for the mentor and mentee for their relationship and how an individual's needs are to be met. Here are some schemes for LIS professionals at a national level:

CILIP	*http://www.cilip.org.uk/*
ALA	*http://www.ala.org/*
ALIA	*http://www.alia.org.au/*
LIANZA	*http://www.lianza.org.nz/*
AIIP	*http://www.aiip.org/*

If you work in a large concern like an academic library or a large public sector organisation then they may operate mentoring programmes either officially or unofficially. Your first step is to speak to your line manager or direct supervisor and ask about opportunities for getting a mentor. Don't be surprised if such a scheme is not confined to the library. When I worked in the private sector I had mentors who worked in different aspects of the business and were economists or statisticians or surveyors.

There is also a route for a more informal process. This can be more difficult to manage as the rules and guidelines have not yet been written and more of the onus will fall to the mentee – that is you. You must think about this situation carefully and how it would work in a practical and effective way. Some of the questions below may help you to think more about it before you seek out a mentor.

- Do you have personal ambition and are ready to take charge of your career?

- Do you recognise that someone in your industry could provide perspective?

- Do you have a willingness to learn from fellow professionals?

- Do you have quite clear goals?

- Do you want to reflect on and analyse your career and/or goals?

At this moment in time I have a couple of people who help me on an informal basis. One is a senior manager in the healthcare sector and the other is an academic. Both are involved in the LIS industry but in different sectors and only one is a LIS professional. I have relied on both at different times for advice and help with my career. I try to get as much out of my meetings with them as possible and prepare well for when we get together.

Remember mentors are giving up time to help you. Time is a precious commodity so respect that. Here are some of my tips for having a mentor in a more informal set-up.

- This is a two-way relationship.

- If you are having a short meeting be prepared.

- Produce a short agenda on what you want to talk about. It also gives your mentor some ideas on what the subject matters and issues will be in advance of the meeting.

- Make sure that you have thought about the issue or problem and take ideas with you. You can use this book to help formulate this. Don't go into this blindly with just a basic idea and hope that someone else will take responsibility and solve your problems.

- Do your homework and apply it. What is the point in learning if you don't apply it?

Stage 2: Reflection

Now that we have explored the reflective stage and the questions you can ask yourself, it's time to explore the practical application for you. This next stage is to use Checklist 3.2 which will help you reflect on and understand what makes you brilliant. Again if you are finding this difficult, then enlist a friend, a colleague or a mentor. You may copy and re-use the checklist as many times as you need.

Stage 3: Not everything is always peachy in LIS world

Hands up if there are any of us that have never had a situation where things have gone wrong? Good, I see you are all still there. Everyone has had times in their past when they wished they had been more prepared, had anticipated the situation better and had worked out a solution before it

Checklist 3.2 Reflecting on what makes you brilliant

Use this checklist yourself and also ask colleagues, mentors and friends to fill it in and compare the results. You can circle as many traits as you would like and also add more if you find some are missing.

Type of person

Circle the type of person

- Ideas
- Leader
- Finisher

- Details
- Creative

When people talk about you what traits and skills do they consider?

Remember you can add to this list too. Circle the traits and skills

- Considerate
- Organised
- Energetic
- Enthusiastic
- Positive outlook
- Problem-solver
- Listener
- Researcher
- Caring
- Insightful
- Self-aware
- Good writer
- Priority management and goals setting
- Scheduling projects

- Calm
- Negotiator
- Financial and budgetary skills
- Data analysis
- Leader
- Manager
- Motivator
- Diplomacy
- Gets the job done
- Brilliant ideas person
- Strategic
- Multitasker
- Wise
- Kind
- Finisher

came to a crisis, leaving them feeling like a complete idiot, heavily criticised and embarrassed with the situation still unresolved. The result of this can be bad and negative feelings that can lead to unhappiness, frustration and perhaps anger which can stop us from moving forward.

So how can we deal effectively with these situations right now? After all, nobody in their right mind wants to go through the same experience again. The question of the truth or sweeping matters under the carpet comes up again, but at the same time don't take the blame for things that were not your fault. One of the most important things I have learned as a LIS professional is pragmatism. I have learned to be much more pragmatic about situations as I get older. Sure, I still get annoyed about some things, but I don't carry the baggage any more. It really can weigh you down.

Once again, this section involves introspection and reflection on your part so I have developed Checklist 3.3 specifically to help you understand and process these situations. Being the average person making more than enough mistakes I have used this checklist on many occasions. Here are some of the tips I have learned about how to handle things differently.

- Listen to your gut feeling.

- Listen carefully when dealing with people. I have found that making my mind up too quickly when someone is talking (and I am not really listening) can cause problems later.

- Understand that sometimes there are rules to the game within an organisation. Decide whether you want to play them. It may be time to move on.

- Always ask for help, even if you feel you should know what to do.

Checklist 3.3 Where did it go wrong?

Use this checklist to identify situations where things did not go well, your role, the outcome and how you may have handled it differently on reflection.

Summarise the situation

What was your role?

What was the outcome of the situation?

With reflection how may you have handled it differently?

What did you learn about yourself and the situation?
Include tips for better handling of people or situations.

Now all that is in the past ... so move on!

- Never pretend you know what you are doing, especially when you are 'all at sea'.

- Prioritise work and identify the different priorities.

- Learn to say no.

- Resist the temptation to react to situations.

- Don't get pulled into other people's arguments.

- Own up to making mistakes or accepting the blame.

- Understand that sometimes you did your best in that situation.

- Understand that sometimes you are not the right fit for a job.

- Your health, whether it is physical or mental, is important and always takes precedence.

- Events happening in your personal life do have a bearing on your work life, e.g. births, deaths, illness, relationships. Sometimes they will stop you in your tracks so don't apologise for feeling that sometimes life is 'not so great'.

Stage 3: Reflection

This section will help you work through situations that left you feeling unhappy or frustrated. Once again work through this with a colleague, friend or mentor.

- Identify disappointments or situations where things went wrong.
- Did you contribute to the situation? What was your role?
- Reflect on how you may have handled the situation differently. Isn't hindsight great?
- Write down your tips for handling situations in the future.
- You can photocopy and reuse the checklist as many times as you need.

The next stage in moving on with your career

Up to this point in the chapter we have audited ourselves and our LIS career using the three-stage plan and accompanying checklists. This now forms the foundation and basis of why we want to be library and information professionals and how we can achieve this. The rest of the book builds on this key information about yourself and looks at what job options there are, starting or moving up in the industry, attitudes to getting the best out of working, tools to help us manage and deliver our goals and managing continuing professional development.

Reflection and understanding for this chapter

- You understand the importance of the three-stage plan.
- You have a clearer understanding of your career to date.
- You understand what is important to you personally.
- You have a better understanding of your assets and skills.
- You reflected on when things went wrong and how you could have changed the situation.
- You understand the role that a mentor can play in shaping your career.
- You are better placed to move forward in your career.

Further reading

Brine, A. (2005) *Continuing Professional Development: A Guide for Information Professionals.* Oxford: Chandos.

Bruce, A. (2007) *Be Your Own Mentor*. New York: McGraw-Hill Professional.

Dority, G.K. (2006) *Rethinking Information Work: A Career Guide for Librarians and Other Information Professionals*. Westport, CT: Libraries Unlimited.

Houghton, A. (2005) *Finding Square Holes*. Carmarthen: Crown House Publishing.

4

Check out the view – the LIS landscape

After you have read this chapter you will:

- have a better understanding of the size of the library and information industry sector;
- have an appreciation for the variety of work that the LIS professional can do whether traditional, non-traditional or hybrid.

Introduction

Why would anyone want to work in the information and library industry? Why would they not? I am in complete agreement with Dennie Heye when he reminded us in his book, *Characteristics of the Successful Twenty-First Century Information Professional*, that we are living in an 'information centric world' and with our skills and expertise we are key players in companies, organisations and indeed society. To further complement what Dennie says, I would like to offer in this chapter a rethink of what the information and library sector has to offer and the huge variety of skills sets it requires for the LIS professional. Indeed, having library and information skills and qualifications can take you across many different industry sectors and open up work in many traditional, non-traditional and hybrid career roles. In fact you will find careers and jobs are more diverse, specialised and different than you may ever have thought. Would you consider a job as a Knowledge Spa Manager, a job I saw advertised over this last year?

Even if you have been working in the LIS sector for a few years you may want to see where else your skills may be utilised. Indeed, you may have been struggling recently to locate roles, as many job titles don't use the words library or information in them. For example, you may have niche subject experience such as media or health or engineering but want to use your more generic research and information management skills, so would you consider a role such as 'research analyst' for a worldwide consultancy group? Or you may find that your have very broad generic skills such as teaching/training in an academic library and want to utilise these in a more specific way such as with community outreach literacy work for young adults. Perhaps your current job as a cataloguer in the media sector has mutated into a more technical IT field – what about diversifying into information architecture and taxonomy construction engineering. This chapter will not deal with the sometimes 'silly' job titles that appear, but it does ask you to delve deeper into what these jobs are actually asking for in terms of skills and competencies.

As previously stated, in today's job market you will not always see the term librarian, library or information professional used to describe jobs that you, as a person with information skills, can actually do. This obviously can cause some problems for the LIS professional, and on scant or uninformed research it could actually suggest that the LIS industry is shrinking. This I believe is far from the truth and requires a different perspective. In an appendix at the end of this chapter I have provided a list of jobs available that I researched on one particular day. The purpose of this list is to provide a snapshot in time of what could potentially be available to you. You will see that the list is diverse and on first glance it is not immediate how a librarian or information professional could do some of these jobs.

Where to start and what to do can be a challenge when you decide to move into the LIS industry. It is also a challenge for professionals already working in the industry whether they should stay in the sector in which they are currently employed or make a move elsewhere. The first thing to recognise is that we all arrive in the industry having trod a different path, and we all come into the industry for different reasons. So first of all, congratulate yourself on knowing your own mind and your reasons for wanting to be part of this industry. If you still do not feel comfortable with this yet then revisit Chapters 2 ('Your LIS career I presume?') and 3 ('It's all about you'). They will give you a better handle on what you want from a job in the information sector, what interests you, what skills you have and how you want to manage your career. Most importantly, they also ask why are you in the LIS industry?

This chapter is intended to help you navigate through the industry landscape by suggesting that we should be guided not by job titles but by the skills and competencies that we as information professionals have by the bucket load.

Education and training

There are so many different career paths into the LIS sector, each with their own educational requirements. However, you can start out at many different levels: straight from high school, after a first degree or following a specialised postgraduate degree. But in order to achieve professional status you must either have a postgraduate qualification from an accredited (by your country's professional association) university course or become a full member of your professional association.

Wherever you are in the world you should make your first positive step by contacting the professional association that supports the library and information services profession in your country. All LIS professional associations are geared up to provide expert guidance and practical help in entering the profession and any educational requirements you may require.

Here are some links to get you started:

- Chartered Institute of Library and Information Professionals (CILIP): *http://www.cilip.org.uk/*
- Library Association of Ireland: *http://www2.libraryassociation .ie/*
- American Library Association: *http://www.ala.org/*
- Canadian Library Association: *http://www.cla.ca/*
- Australian Library Association: *http://www.alia.org.au/*
- New Zealand (LIANZA): *http://www.lianza.org.nz/*

Broad library and information strands

There are some key broad strands that make up the possible configuration of LIS careers. Other books are dedicated to this topic and as a result this book will not replicate this work. However, this chapter seeks to open up the industry under the following broad headings.

- *Archives*. These are records that are no longer currently in use but could have a perceived historical or social value. However, that does not mean to say that they cannot be accessed immediately. For example, the BBC has always had working television and news archives in the UK and some of these are now in digitised collections. This archive is at the heart of many of the BBC's moneymaking ventures. Of course, many countries have national libraries, but any kind of collection will have an archive.

- *Competitive intelligence*. How do you find out what a competitor organisation is up to and what their longer- or shorter-term plans are? You may have an interest in a particular person, such as appointing them as a director of your organisation. Information that is in the public domain or published data can be analysed to provide intelligence for making decisions about competition. News, company reports and industry and sector market reports are generally used in this type of work.

- *Corporate memory*. One big problem for organisations is assessing what they know as an organisation. This includes the documents, records and archives produced by an organisation. Consider also the knowledge in an employee's head – what happens when that employee moves on to pastures green?

- *Data management*. What do you do with bits of information so that people can find and re-use it? For example, imagine you are trying to digitise a television archive for a variety of different client groups such as the public, for internal re-use within the organisation and also for sale to outside clients. What if you needed to track, as an organisation, your key physical assets and all the related capital investment expenditure? You would require database planning, analysis, design, implementation, maintenance, metadata management and data mining.

- *Document management.* This is increasingly a common problem in organisations: what do you do with the vast amounts of information and documents that are created daily within a business? There is also the question of freedom of information, so depending on the legislation in your country, there could be an obligation to make available or provide certain facts and figures. Information could be part of 'business as usual', but also relate to project work and other outputs. In any business the ability to manage and control documents and information is vital. A key problem is how to find documents and how to store them in order that workflow is not disrupted. Storage of information is still a key question even in the electronic age.

- *Information architecture.* This has somewhat different meanings depending on what you are reading, but there are broad headings that are common to all with regard to designing organisation, navigation, labelling and search mechanisms. Library systems, content management systems, web development, programming and technical writing are all examples and are often found in shared environments.

- *Information audit.* How well does information flow in your organisation? Is there replication in the production of information rather than sharing? Do different initiatives, when studied, actually seek to produce the same outputs? Are there dead ends for information where they are left hanging? What about the behaviours, attitudes and practices of your employees? Is your organisation and/or service designed with the criteria which constitute success and the benefits which will be realised in mind?

- *Information policy*. How do we handle information and what do we do with it? Routine methods (in some cases a step-by-step guide) of handling and treating information can be set down which can also be used to review current information practices in order to achieve particular objectives. For example, if you offer a literature search service in a clinical setting you may have different levels of search available with associated turnaround times such as three days, one week or two weeks. Suppose you have a service level agreement to provide a pilot for a new LIS service, a fast turnaround same-day literature service – what aspects of the library service policy would you have to change?

- *KM (knowledge management)*. This is the ability to harness and control knowledge within an organisation, e.g. sharing it, managing it, storing it and mapping it. This works in partnership with corporate memory in that its purpose is to decide what is useful.

- *Libraries*. Libraries themselves each come with a special set of skills some of which may be required more in particular settings than in others. For example, in an academic setting, skills in information literacy and teaching are useful, while in a workplace specialist library research analyst skills work well, and in a public library a customer-service approach is highly prized.

- *Records management*. Consider how many organisations have records of business transactions to manage in terms of accumulation, handling, storage, organisation, governance and accountability. Can an organisation say what its business is, what its expectations are, what evidence there is of outputs, and can it verify its performance and perhaps even its impact, be that economic or the realisation of benefits?

- *Strategic information management.* All organisations need this kind of information to ensure their survival, and the most successful organisations are always thinking about the future today. What kind of information could be used to further develop a plan or goals for that unique organisation? It is a highly prized ability to find relevant information, synthesise it and use it to guide development.

Traditional library

There are a number of major library sectors that fall into the traditional category and are probably the place you would consider it most likely to find a job as a librarian. This includes public, school and academic libraries. If it is important that you are involved in a public sector environment then the traditional library may be for you, although I must warn you not all the jobs fit into the traditional mould.

Public libraries

Public libraries serve communities and can be quite different in nature and size depending on their geographic location and purpose. For example, in the major UK city in which I live, Glasgow in Scotland, we have a world-renowned reference library (the Mitchell Library), city libraries and also community libraries. These provide a variety of historical archives, support learning in the community and are a focus for specific groups such as youth, adults, parents and the elderly. Even infants and the very young are supported with storytelling and singing groups. It is commonly reported that many librarians were attracted to the LIS industry because of their affection for the local public library and access to books and information. There is also the idealistic notion of the 'people's university' and opportunities for life-long learning, and that by working in a community library you could quite possibly be in a position to change someone's life.

There are many romantic images of public libraries as places of peace, nurture, possibilities and calmness, and long may that continue. But public libraries are changing and the remit of this book does not include a debate over whether that is a good or bad thing; if you want to take part in that debate you need to read elsewhere. However, if library users are leading developments in how people want to interact with information now and have an expectation for entertainment and learning environments then this could change the way we think about the public library. Learning centres, access to the Internet, DVDs and CDs as well as film-making for youths, massage for babies and, yes, even borrowing hard-copy books – each public library (or city/county/community library) will have its own remit to provide the most appropriate services for its users. Think about the level at which you want to interact with the public, for example as a community librarian providing youth services in a challenging environment or by archiving local history in a city reference library.

School libraries

School libraries are part of the school system which, depending on where you live in the world, can last from age 4 up to age 18. School types can also vary, for example from infant schools to middle schools to high schools. Some schools can accommodate pupils all the way from 4 until 18, though this is more common in the private school sector.

For some children this could be the first experience (or in some cases the only experience) that they will have of libraries, therefore you do have the potential to make a huge difference to someone's life. Working with children can be challenging, exciting, exhausting, but if you feel that you have the temperament for and interest in working with this group then it can be particularly rewarding. Working in the school environment may mean that you could be the only information professional, perhaps working solo, and there is no doubt that 'multitasking' will be reflected in your job description. Here are some of the roles you will be involved in:

- demonstration of reference materials;
- information literacy skills training;
- research skills: identifying, evaluating and using appropriate resources either in print or e-format;
- IT skills: demonstrating e-tools and the Internet to both students and teachers;
- collection and acquisitions: identifying and acquiring appropriate materials and working with teaching colleagues to support their classes and the curriculum;
- management: implementing strategy and priorities in line with school plans, managing and delivering projects and supervising administrative support (if you have any);
- everyday operational: general enquiries, shelving, circulation management.

Academic libraries

Academic libraries can be found in colleges and universities, their users being students, staff and faculty members. Larger universities usually have several libraries dedicated to particular subject specialities such as medicine, music, art, engineering and business. It is common for librarians in university libraries to have high levels of subject specialism. However, they can also have more generic skills sets and a more hybrid set of competencies (see later in this chapter for more on hybrid librarians).

This sector opens up many opportunities for the librarian/information professional. It is generally a highly structured workplace with many levels of bureaucracy. There are opportunities for getting involved in a variety of work and a range of projects and you will work with a large and diverse group of fellow professionals.

There are a number of categories of jobs in academic libraries such as:

- *user services* – including reference, research, community, bibliographic instruction and circulation;
- *technical services* – including acquisitions, collection development, serials management, processing (cataloguing), shelving and managing IT;
- *administrative services* – including personnel management, budgeting, staff development, leadership and organisational management.

More information for the traditional sector

You can further explore these sectors by accessing information through the various professional associations such as the Chartered Institute of Library and Information Professionals and American Library Association:

- ALA: *http://www.ala.org/*
- CILIP sector guides: *http://www.cilip.org.uk/*

Non-traditional (special) library

The great news is that the library and information sector is huge and for many who do not see themselves in the traditional library field the non-traditional or special library field has almost never-ending possibilities.

There are opportunities to work in libraries or information services where the work is focused in a specialism or niche area. This may include private or public sector organisations, hospitals, prisons, the defence industry, government departments, the legal sector, museums and art, media, music, engineering, architecture and also special collections. Generally, you will be working in a small unit supporting a variety of other professionals in that field. For example, I worked in a business information service for a worldwide consulting group supporting economists, financial analysts and planning developers. Although these libraries may have a non-traditional role they may have a recognisably traditional setting such as enquiry work, current awareness, training and teaching, reference work, collection development and document delivery.

You may find yourself working in a service for very specific groups in the population such as the voluntary (non-profit) sector. For example, your organisation may support people with specific health needs or medical conditions, specific age groups such as the elderly or children, or particular racial/religious groups.

The special libraries sector is vast and provides almost limitless possibilities for work. Many of the national professional associations support or represent this sector via their special interest groups. As a starter you should become familiar with their information sources.

Hybrid information professionals

The emergence of IT and its convergence with information management in the LIS sector has often been quoted as a threat to the sector, but I would like to suggest that it has actually had the opposite effect and has opened up the job market in a way we could not have imagined. With my experience of working in libraries it is often quite difficult to separate IT questions from information questions generally as the technology is the delivery agent. IT allows for greater collaborative working and delivery and sharing of information, but at the root there are still fundamental questions about information management. This has led, either by design or evolution, to the development of the hybrid information professional.

This development is particularly relevant in the academic sector and the role has expanded beyond traditional subject support and collection development and management. You may see some jobs such as:

- Learning/teaching technologist
- Informatics
- Web/intranet manager
- Systems librarian
- E-resources advisor/manager
- E-strategy manager
- IT support manager
- Technical services librarian (sounds a little outdated now).

There are some specific skills that are generally looked for or required for working in this area. In particular some in the academic sector are moving away from subject specialities or the need to have a subject qualification. However, the key skills requirements seem to be:

- teaching and user education skills and experience;
- experience and understanding of information literacy theory and practice;
- IT skills beyond the basics;
- good customer service skills;
- communication skills;
- ability to work in virtual learning environments.

Other types of library and information work

There are some other options that you can pursue in the library and information sector. This includes library and information science teaching/instruction and research, working for an information vendor, publishing and working as an independent LIS professional. To find out more about working independently you should work through Chapter 12.

Reflection and understanding for this chapter

This chapter will have demonstrated to you:

- that the LIS professional has a large industry to choose from;
- that the variety of jobs is enormous;
- the types of job or sector that may interest you.

Appendix 4.1: A snapshot selection of jobs that were being advertised on 16 September 2008

Acquisitions and metadata
specialist
Archives assistant
Assistant librarian
Business development
officer
Cataloguer
Clinical effectiveness
officer/librarian
Communications officer
Community programming
officer
Conservator
Content manager
Curator
Database administrator
Digital content
officer/manager
Document support/delivery
manager
e-Content advisor
e-Learning support
officer/librarian
e-Resources specialist
Editor
Information detective
Information manager
Intranet manager
Intranet resources officer

Know-how content coordinator
Knowledge executive manager
Knowledge transfer manager
Learning development
coordinator
Librarian
Literacy worker
Market and competitive
intelligence manager
Medical education resource
centre manager
Medical information specialist
Operations manager
Project manager
Reader advisor
Records manager/specialist
Records officer/manager
Repository officer
Research associate
Research/information analyst
Researcher
Retrospective cataloguer
Service innovation officer
Storyteller
Study support assistant
Study support manager
Subject/faculty librarian
Web developer
Workflow controller

Further reading

Baofu, P. (2008) *The Future of Information Architecture.* Oxford: Chandos.

Batley, S. (2007) *Information Architecture for Information Professionals.* Oxford: Chandos.

Bowman, J.H. (ed.) (2007) *British Librarianship and Information Work 2001–2005.* Aldershot: Ashgate:

Brophy, P. (2005) *The Academic Library.* London: Facet.

Cerney, R. et al. (2006) *Outstanding Library Service to Children.* Chicago: American Library Association.

Dority, G. Kim (2006) *Rethinking Information Work. A Career Guide for Librarians and Other Information Professionals.* Westport, CT: Libraries Unlimited.

Gordon, R.S. (2008) *What's the Alternative? Career Options for Librarians and Information Pros.* Medford, NJ: Information Today.

Goulding, A. (2008) *Public Libraries in the 21st Century.* Aldershot: Ashgate.

Harvey, T. and Chance, C. (2003) *The Role of the Legal Information Officer.* Oxford: Chandos.

Hawamdeh, S. (2003) *Knowledge Management: Cultivating Knowledge Professionals.* Oxford: Chandos.

Heye, D. (2006) *Characteristics of the Successful Twenty-First Century Information Professional.* Oxford: Chandos.

Higgins, S.E. (2007) *Youth Services and Public Libraries.* Oxford: Chandos.

Hughes-Hassell, S. and Wheelock, A. (2001) *The Information-Powered School.* Chicago: American Library Association.

Levy, P. and Roberts, S. (eds) *Developing the New Learning Environment.* London: Facet.

Lidman, T. (2008) *Scientific Libraries: Past Developments and Future Changes*. Oxford: Chandos.

McMenemy, D. (2008) *The Public Library*. London: Facet.

McMenemy, D. and Rooney-Browne, C. (2008) *The Public Library Training Handbook*. London: Facet.

Maxwell, N.K. (2006) *Sacred Stacks: The Higher Purposes of Libraries and Librarianship*. Chicago: American Library Association.

Murphy, C. (2005) *Competitive Intelligence. Gathering, Analyzing and Putting It to Work*. Aldershot: Ashgate.

Myburgh, S. (2005) *The New Information Professional: How to Thrive in the Information Age Doing What You Love*. Oxford: Chandos.

Oldroyd, M. (2004) *Developing Academic Library Staff for Future Success*. London: Facet.

Townsend Kane, L. (2003) *Straight from the Stacks: A First-hand Guide to Careers in Library and Information Science*. Chicago: American Library Association.

Usherwood, B. (2007) *Excellence and Equity in the Public Library: Why Ignorance Is Not Our Heritage*. Aldershot: Ashgate.

Walter, V.A. (2001) *Children and Libraries: Getting It Right*. Chicago: American Library Association.

Part 2

Everyday tools for taking charge of your career

5

Tips for keeping up with business as usual and managing change

After you have read this chapter you will understand how you can make some changes to your daily life that will lead to big rewards for your career. Sometimes this is also called continuing professional development but I like to call it keeping up with business as usual and managing change. It includes:

- embracing change;
- making a commitment;
- attitude;
- being more creative;
- working outside your comfort zone;
- checking out the neighbour's garden;
- hard and soft thinking;
- being sociable and networking;
- planning to succeed and goal setting;
- work–life balance;
- professional reading;
- using a journal.

Introduction

This book provides a variety of tools and techniques for taking charge of your LIS career and getting the results that you want. Some of the tools and techniques are more focused on the medium and longer-length project, but there are some things that you can do on a more regular basis to manage the daily 'operational running and fine tuning' of you, the LIS professional. I was thinking about calling this chapter 'continuing professional development' but I did not think I could encapsulate all the ideas that are useful in taking charge of your career.

The fact that you are already reading this book suggests to me that you are doing something practical about your career and want a stake in any decisions about it. Maybe you have been ignoring this for some time and already know (perhaps deep down) that this experience is a career limiting option. Believe me, I have been there. At any point in your career there are only ever two options or decisions to make and they are really simple:

1. Stay where you are and do nothing.

2. Move on and change.

Don't worry, this chapter is not just about positive thinking. A cheerful and happy mindset are good but they will not be the only things that will help you manage and direct your goals. There are quite a lot of things we can do on a daily basis to get more from ourselves as LIS professionals and our work, and it is my belief that we can be hindered on a daily basis by the way we act, think, ignore, interact, plan and look after ourselves. This chapter looks at some key ideas for changing our attitudes, getting momentum and being generally happier in a professional way.

Coping with change

There are usually a number of reactions to the word 'change' – fear, suspicion, anger, annoyance, upset, nervousness. Does the idea of change send a shiver up your back? On the other hand, think about how you would feel if *you* were in control – happy powerful, excited? Most of us experience change through someone else, which makes us feel powerless and lacking control. When we think about taking charge of your LIS career it is essentially about change within you, and the word 'you' is underlined and in bold. That means that you control it, so should you fear something that you already control?

Becoming one with 'change' is about changing your own mindset and taking a chance with something you can control. Remember, 'you will make zero percent of the shots you don't take' (Michael Jordan, the US basketball player), so why not put yourself in charge of your own change?

When coping with change you need to understand and reduce the risks to yourself. Here are some of the tips I have used to help myself understand the situation a little better.

- Get some perspective (perhaps some help from other LIS professionals) and understand what is going on in your life and, most importantly, the LIS industry. Chapter 2 ('Your LIS career I presume?') and Chapter 3 ('It's all about you') will help with this.

- Work out what really matters in your life and get excited about it, whether it's personal or professional. Believe me, being excited or looking forward to something (even something a little scary like writing this book) does make it easier to handle. Chapter 2 ('Your LIS career I presume?') and Chapter 3 ('It's all about you') will help with this.

- Get really clear on what you want to happen and goals you may have. Chapter 6 ('Making the time for managing your career') and Chapter 7 ('Taking charge using project management as a tool') will help.

- Get excited about your own success, whatever you define success to be.

- Be passionate about what you do – and that's not about being married to the job. People can spot 'fake passion' a mile off. Consistently deliver and care about what you do. Chapter 2 ('Your LIS career I presume?'), Chapter 3 ('It's all about you') and Chapter 4 ('Check out the view – the LIS landscape') will help with this.

- Work out your allies professionally. These could be fellow professionals in the LIS sector, professionals working in other organisational departments or professionals who work in your preferred LIS sector.

- Ask for help from experienced and important people. Read through Chapter 3 ('It's all about you').

- Expect the unexpected and that you will go off course. This is life, not an exact science. I have learned more about myself on the journey than on reaching the destination.

- You will be out of your comfort zone, but it will feel good (though perhaps only after the event).

- Be persistent and stay committed.

Are you a commitment-phobe?

One of the overriding factors that will help you achieve your goals and objectives is your level of commitment and it is this single item that generally derails your ambitions.

I believe that most people use the word 'commitment' inappropriately: it is generally considered to be a noun ... a promise, a dedication. However, I like to think of it as more of a verb, a doing word, an action word. When I use the word commitment I immediately think of tasks and programmes. I make a plan to get where I want and use it to keep me focused, and more importantly I update my progress and see where I am. It's not always good news, but if I am being true to my commitment I will try to take more action. It is my experience that before I thought of commitment in this way I could easily become ambivalent about what I had hoped to do and opportunities could easily be missed. Very soon ideas and plans would just slip away engulfed by the daily 'stuff' I had to do. So start thinking about commitment in terms of the verb rather than the noun.

Attitude

Have a think about what your attitude is to most things. Consider this scenario. An opportunity has presented itself and you have been invited to give a talk at a national library conference for your professional association. However, it is in six weeks' time. What is your reply? Choose 1 or 2:

1. Only a month or so away, so I would have to put a lot of work in and it's just a one-off event. I could maybe do something later on in the year. I am not even sure I would get away from the library. The manager would never give me permission. I was thinking I may take a holiday then and I would probably have to take two trains to get there.

2. Only a month or so away, that is quite a tight deadline. However, this is a great opportunity and I will check with my boss that I can get away from the library and make

sure I can cover commitments in my personal life. I could move some of my work commitments around. I will ask my boss if I could have some time for preparation and in return I could make a short presentation to all staff in the library and write it up for a journal. I am quite nervous, as I have never done anything like this before. Perhaps a friend who does a lot of public speaking could help me with it. Somebody must have confidence that I have something interesting to say.

Do you see the difference in replies? Both answers are from a person who gets nervous and who is shy. How do I know? Because both of them have been me at different points in my LIS career. Both of these attitudes and beliefs shaped my career at different points, and I will leave you to work out what scenario had the best outcome for me. Be prepared to take a risk and be conscious about beliefs and attitudes that may be holding you back.

> ## Reflection
>
> Consider your attitude in terms of some chances or opportunities that have come your way as a LIS professional. What was the opportunity? What decisions did you have to make? What choice did you make? With hindsight did you make the best choice?

Start the creative process

Let me start by saying that I never considered myself to be a creative person or that it was really a requirement for life as a LIS professional, but reflecting back over the years I think I was confusing being artistic with being creative. For the record – and in case anyone is interested – I can't draw for toffee. However, I started realising a few years ago that I was actually quite creative in my ideas and suggestions but had been holding back for fear of being wrong or going against the herd. I was interested not just in how problems were solved in the LIS sector but in other industry sectors. Why should we not learn from shop retailers about customer services? Why should we not learn from the music and media industries about branding for users? How can we incorporate transformational leadership styles to encourage more 'buy in' to change? I realised that through the work I was involved in I was questioning, reflecting and planning with service users, clients and colleagues and in doing so unlocking my creative side.

One thing I can guarantee as you work through this book is that it will start to unlock the creativity in you, because this book was piloted on a regular library and information professional (me) and the questions, reflections and planning started my creativity. In fact you may find it difficult to stop thinking creatively and will probably find it flowing into your life generally.

Creativity is something we all have in us – we just need to learn how to unlock its potential. The most important thing you need to know about being creative is that you need to show your ignorance about most things, so sit back and start enjoy being confused by stuff and ask lots of questions. For many years I felt quite uncomfortable not knowing things I felt I should know about (especially as I was a late entrant into the LIS sector) and I am sure we all feel pressurised to find answers to problems and come up with solutions. It is easy sometimes and more comfortable to look at LIS examples that have already been tried and tested. However, being creative takes practice, and it is not a quick-fix solution. Forget the notion of getting it right the first time. Some problems take time to unpick and more often than not I think up a variety of solutions. Most of the solutions I work through will be 'rubbish' or 'unworkable', but from the thought process I start to understand and see a way through. It's all about practising, using different methods to work through an issue and all the possible solutions. You will then start to see the 'wood from the trees'.

Reflection

Think about a recent problem you were trying to solve and how you may have been more creative about it. Write down as many different ways you could potentially solve it as you can (even if they sound daft). Then you need to get some perspective on your idea, so take it outside your ideas stage by involving a friend, a colleague, the library team or your department. You may be surprised by the reaction – for real creativity you will always need input not only from fellow workers and professionals, but also from people unconnected with the LIS sector.

Asking the 'why' and 'what'

There are two ways in which you can ask yourself questions and both will have an impact on how you feel and behave. If you ask yourself the 'why' question all the time you will soon find out how negative a situation can be. Why is my job in academic libraries going nowhere? Why do I continually find myself spread thinly across operational and management duties and service development? Why did I never get that taxonomy project finished? Why is she managing to do the same librarian job as me and leave on time every night? I would like to suggest that a more useful way of working (and perhaps for your own sanity) is to ask more of the 'what' question. What would I have to do to get my LIS career where I want it? What tools can I use to make sure I prioritise my operational library duties? What if I used the principles of project management to deliver the marketing for the new literature search service project? What changes could I make to my work planning so that I could leave every night on time? Do you see how using different language can make you feel? It's a more positive way to deal with issues and working out solutions.

Reflection

Make a list of 'why' questions that you have as a LIS professional. Now leave a space between each question. When you have completed the 'why' questions, go back through and change them into 'what' questions. Re-read both sets of questions and compare how you felt reading the 'why' in comparison to the 'what'.

Working outside your LIS comfort zone

As LIS professionals we are keen to create specialisms and niche areas for ourselves – you could be a clinical librarian, a social sciences faculty librarian, a cataloguer, a literacy specialist. I could go on, but I am sure you get the picture. As a result I think it makes us less likely to step out of our roles, even although we know it is good to vary our exposure. Even if we get involved in specialist groups, committees or other events it is likely that we will still stay in our broad subject areas. But how would you feel about talking to a group of LIS professionals from another LIS industry sector or outside the industry? What is your reaction as a faculty librarian to managing a project that converges your university's library service with several IT departments? How would you feel about taking a recent library project and getting it published in a peer reviewed library and information journal? There are many things that can take us out of our specialisms and comfort zone, but to do so on a regular basis provides momentum and energy to go on and achieve more. Also, as the old adage goes, it gets easier the more you practise.

> ## Reflection
>
> Look out for or think about a situation that, when presented to you, will take you out of your comfort zone. How does this make you feel and what is your natural instinct? If this is a really scary prospect for you, then start by doing something small (but different), for example agreeing to do a small training session for users for one of your LIS colleagues, taking the minutes of the next staff meeting, reporting at the next staff meeting on an interesting article you have read. To take things a stage further, go to a library and information professional event alone that you would not normally go to. Be prepared to talk about what you do and why you have come.

Checking out the neighbour's garden – non-LIS input

I don't believe that as a professional industry we go about planning to be arrogant and self-indulgent. However, sometimes I see very little thought given by the LIS industry to looking at what is going on in other non-LIS industry sectors. Given that I have already said that it is very difficult to keep up to date and abreast of changes in the LIS sector it would incredible that I am now suggesting that we LIS professionals consider what is going on in other industries.

However, what I am suggesting is that we consider evidence from other industries on key areas of career development. Are you interested in leadership skills? Then learn from some of the transformational change and leadership examples for the retail and utilities sector. You want to develop a more customer-focused service? Then learn about 'knowing your user' from the retail sector. The next time you are researching for more information for your own career development, think about looking at the issue from a different perspective and you may learn that we have more in common with other industries or organisations than you think.

I have worked as a clinical librarian and there are a couple of best-practice procedures that have been adapted from completely different industries to the medical sector. Could you ever imagine that Formula 1 car racing would have an impact on heart transplant procedures and care of the patient? What about risk management processes and procedures for the accident and emergency room?

Reflection

Think about a LIS project or career issue you have and how some outside perspective may help. In the first instance try and find someone outside your organisation that may be able to provide perspective and a different viewpoint. Secondly, look for someone outside the LIS sector who can offer some other perspective. You could contact someone who wrote an interesting article you have read or heard at a conference. Start researching the issue and identify a person or organisation that could help you. If you feel that contacting the person is outside your comfort zone at the moment, then develop a portfolio of best practice, advice or tips.

Hard (sore) and soft (easy) thinking

Has this ever happened to you? You are in a cafe on a Saturday having coffee (or at the gym, on holiday, or even sleeping) when out of nowhere you realise how to get round a problem that has been perplexing you. This is what I call soft or easy thinking. No stress, no hassle, very painless. This is great news, but it seems very rare that we can allow our brains and thought processes to engage in such a fashion.

The usual scenario is we are under pressure to find an answer, come up with solutions and make recommendations. I am sure that all of us at some point have had to endure this situation round a table. This is hard or sore (because I usually get a headache) thinking. Does it work? Yes and no. Is it enjoyable? Usually not. Just like unleashing your creativity, when problem-solving the relevant facts need time to sink in, and you need lots of ideas to just come and go so that you can work through the ridiculous to the fantastic. Impatience with solving a problem or an issue can result in going round in circles and not achieving much, or the decision is made too early and it will become just a quick fix. As an example, suppose you have read this book from cover to cover without engaging with the practice and reflection sections. However, if you do not use the tools and checklists along with the reflective and introspective processes then the book will be quite meaningless. It may inspire you in the short term, but will it actually help to manage your goals in the longer term? Probably not.

It is an easy thing to say, 'Have an open mind'. But it can be quite hard to do. I have found the easiest way to do this is to try and expose yourself to different opinions. For example, a few years ago I joined a committee in order to encounter a new situation. Initially I found it incredibly hard and even considered giving it up after a few months – it wasn't the people or the organisation, it was me. I was totally out of my comfort zone and having to think and behave in a different way. The break came when I decided just to listen to what others were saying, think about the big picture, go home and sleep on it. In many ways it has taught me to resist the temptation for the quick fix and to have a more rounded view of a situation. I am still involved in that committee.

Reflection

Think about a LIS situation where you are having trouble solving the issues and the problems surrounding it – it could be a career situation or not. Take a piece of paper and write down, off the top of your head for the next 5–10 minutes, a summary of the situation and possible actions. For the next seven days revisit this question for only 10–15 minutes (maximum) and add some more ideas – it doesn't matter how much or little you write. It will now be lodged in your brain (somewhere) for attention. When odd ideas start popping into your head or people start giving you information write them down and make a note if you have made connections with things you are reading or other material you are working on. After the seven days see how far you have come with ideas and solutions.

Let's get sociable

Much of what we have been working through in this chapter is about addressing our creative side as LIS professionals. Well, I can tell you that being creative does not work in a vacuum. You cannot do it on your own and I know because I work mainly alone. Let me rephrase that, I work alone but not in isolation. One of the key features of creativity is that you need to be exposed to diversity and for that we need to be more sociable.

I am not a naturally sociable person I said to a good friend recently. She laughed so much she said it hurt. What I was really meaning was that sometimes I get nervous in social and work situations. Well so does everyone she said back.

The one thing that I have learned over the years is to find inspiration in other places. In order to do that you need to be out and about in new places and expose yourself to different perspectives and people, for example through:

- volunteering;
- committee work;
- taking on a project at work;
- writing for publication;
- going to a conference, alone;
- eating in different restaurants;
- turning up at the open classes for salsa dancing;
- taking up a new sport like tennis.

The list is endless, but whatever you do make sure it's sociable and you enjoy it.

LIS professional networking

Up until around five years ago the thought of 'networking' or explicitly making an effort to network filled me with fear as a LIS professional, which in some ways was ridiculous because as an independent I can ill afford not to be known. For me I felt it had connotations of the hard sell, like the car salesman. Then something happened to me and even now it's hard to put a finger on exactly what is was. A crisis of confidence, detachment from the profession, unsure of which road to follow, lethargy, two small babies, exhaustion? All these reasons were valid, but at the back my mind I had some ideas to expand my LIS career and step into the unknown. I shared my ideas with a fellow LIS colleague and she immediately connected me with three people that could provide a broader perspective. This is how I started networking and this was my pivotal moment for getting on track.

Many of us find it difficult to admit we need help or can't work something out on our own. We also know that having a fresh perspective or more information or meeting the right person can really help a situation. I have learned that networking can help bring energy, direction, counsel and in some cases a helping hand to achieve goals. By meeting lots of people in different situations you should also expect to boost your creative juices. I have also learned that it is about relationships, it's not about business cards and it's definitely not about the hard sell.

Networking is a proactive occupation, and with all of us seemingly endlessly busy all the time you can ponder whether there is actually time for this. But also ask yourself, have you ever had a chance meeting with someone and it has affected you in some positive way? Networking is really just about increasing your chances of meeting the right people in the right conditions. The key thing to remember is that there is an element of reciprocity in networking – you need to give something back too. If you are using it to manipulate situations or be selfish about your own needs then this is wrong, and ultimately it will not work for you.

Networking is a process inside and outside an organisation and both are equally important. Generally we think about networking as being an 'out of your organisation' thing. But you can gain a lot from connecting with people inside the organisation you are already in. When

I worked in the consultancy sector I learned much from economists, statisticians and public policy-makers who all had a direct contribution to bettering my success in the work I did in that organisation.

For anyone that knows me personally they will tell you that I can 'talk for Scotland'. The thing is that it is mainly a defence mechanism for being quite shy and uneasy in social situations. I like to practise (code for not sure what is going on) at being shy quite a lot and hate the silence that comes with it, so I talk. Through meeting on a regular basis with quite a variety of people this has definitely helped with this aspect of my personality. Although I am still essentially shy I like people and like to feel part of whatever is going on, and hopefully my talking is more coherent and thoughtful now.

To make networking work for you, you need to be aware of what you want to get out of it. In the story I told you about myself I was looking for help to jumpstart my career in the library profession. I already had some ideas but I needed to share them with others and hear what they had to say. As you will see throughout this book if you have no clear goals then you are very likely not going to achieve anything. You can use Chapter 3 ('It's all about you') and Chapter 7 ('Taking charge using project management as a tool') to help you with this further.

If you are having a hard time getting going or have just forgot how to do this as it's been a while then take advantage of some of the ready-made networks available to you. After taking a couple of years out in quiet isolation with two babies (in close succession) I took advantage of my personal membership of the Scottish Health Information Network (SHINe) to start interacting with fellow LIS professionals at events and became involved in some of the working groups, initially at quite a slow pace. If you are a member of a LIS professional association then this is an

---

Reflection and tips

Here are some ideas that you should think about and practise for networking.

- Share your goals with someone and ask their advice on how you can move forward. More often than not they will recommend others to speak to.
- Look for events where you can showcase some of your talents such as conferences or professional association meetings.
- Publish some of your thoughts or ideas or projects you have been working on.
- If you go to a meeting via a contact, then be prepared to be upfront about what you expect from the meeting.
- Be prepared to say what you do and talk about yourself.
- Develop and practise small talk.

---

excellent and straightforward way to meet people and attend events.

Breaking free – work out how to fail?

I will own up immediately and tell you that I borrowed this idea from my husband who works in capital investment in the utilities industry – perhaps he borrowed it from somewhere else, and I have definitely seen it mentioned in Dennie Heye's brilliant book (Heye, 2006). I thought it was so simple yet brilliant that I have been using it now for quite a few years successfully. He told me of a situation in which he and some colleagues were trying to solve a problem by thinking about what they would have to do in order to fail miserably to deliver a programme costing millions of pounds. People found it so easy to identify the key failure criteria, and I thought I could use the idea myself in my library work. Most of how I manage to achieve milestones or finish work is by first working out how I could fail at it.

For example, 'How could I fail to deliver a Medline training session for a group of health promotion professionals in two months time?' Here are some of the things I could do – some of them seem rather obvious and silly but the list does highlight what I would actually have to do to be successful:

- use an old training programme that was only suitable for qualified information professionals;
- not liaise with the health promotion team managers;
- not use appropriate examples and re-use my examples for the cardiothoracic specialists;
- not write the course and just 'wing it' on the day;
- start writing the course the day before the event;
- have no handouts;
- not book the training room;
- not make sure that we had enough supplies to print off the training pack;
- start brainstorming ideas for the training day three days before the event;
- book a day off on the training session day.

So, by writing down how you can fail, you can easily see the tasks needed to make something work. If I am really stuck on projects or how to move forward I like to use this idea. You will hear more about this technique in Chapter 7 ('Taking charge using project management as a tool').

> ## Reflection
>
> Take a LIS situation involving your career development and work out the criteria for failing. On a sheet of paper work out the steps that would cause you not to deliver this target. For example, imagine you are thinking about promotion and moving into a more managerial role. Here are some of the things that you may write down:
>
> - Never offer to run the weekly library team briefing.
> - Never offer to represent your boss at a faculty meeting.
> - Don't get involved in a library project where you need to manage a team.
> - Never ever research management skills and competencies for the LIS professional or seek out best practice.
> - Don't bother yourself with a course on moving into management available from your professional association.

Tips for successful goal-setting

I am sure that most of you will have set goals for yourself over your lifetime either as an information professional or as a personal endeavour. Some of them may have worked out and some will have failed. Why is that? Why do some goals work out and some not? Here are some ideas which may impact on the outcome of your goals.

- Inspiration and energy: what am I drawn to or curious about? So if your real love is to work in a music library then why are trying to pursue a job in a medical library?

- Doing what you love: if you don't love what you do then don't expect it to love you back.

- Listen to your intuition: are you clear about what you want? Your work may be hectic, perhaps stressful, but you still feel excited and know that you are doing the right thing.

- Trust yourself: trust your abilities without knowing how it will pan out.

There is more about goal-setting and managing goal-setting in Chapter 6 ('Making the time for managing your career') and Chapter 7 ('Taking charge using project management as a tool').

Professional reading

How much information do you have coming at you on a regular basis related to the LIS industry? I am a member of a professional association and a couple of special interest groups. I am also a member of a cooperative library and information health organisation for Scotland and I subscribe to a couple of general industry news journals. On top of all that I am on the mailing list of three specialist librarians for their monthly (quarterly) digests and mailing for nearly all Freepint alerts. That is quite a lot of information coming my way on a monthly basis. Let me tell you, it used to be a lot more.

I pride myself in having always been brilliant at building up portfolios of reading material to help me fill in the gaps in knowledge and keep abreast of the information and library sector. There was one big problem – I never read any of it, but the piles of papers and printouts grew at an exponential rate. Does this sound familiar? I had moved into collection development and archiving without even realising it. When I moved house, which was on average every fours years, I would put it all in a box and take it with me. Obviously such a waste of time, but the hoarder in me thought that I would eventually read the stuff. Eventually I realised that my whole technique was completely flawed, and as an LIS professional I should have spotted that my collection management procedure was never going to work. I was never going to read it, so after my last move five years ago I binned the whole lot, cleared out my office and filing system, and started with a new plan. As a LIS professional we know that all this is just stuff – it is the analysis and synthesis and putting the knowledge into practice that makes it worthwhile in the first place.

The *raison d'être* of having any LIS service lies in being able to provide information, to inform, to help with decision-making and to have an impact – this is quite a biggie for the LIS industry and probably the requirement of a separate book. Suffice it to say the information in the articles, books and blogs were only of interest to me if I dissected the stuff I really wanted and binned the rest. I started thinking of a better way to manage my information – after all I already did this for clients. And as information people we know that the real value of information is what you do with that knowledge.

So as ever I started with the end in mind: why and what did I need to keep up with? Here are some tips that I have worked out:

- Go through all you subscribe to or 'just get' and ask yourself whether you really do need to be getting this and what it adds. Be ruthless and relate this to your general professional requirements but also to specific career wishes you have ongoing.
- If you are either in a niche sector or want to move into such a sector make reading material coming from this sector a priority.

- Always have one general LIS industry news journal/blog/publication to get a general overview of the main features of the industry.

- Read with a motive and intention: if you are serious about a particular subject/sector start by reading and making notes in a journal to build up your knowledge.

- People and themes: sometimes it is more important to know the people working in a sector or specialised area, so build up a picture of who is writing about what and what their main interests are. There are certain people I follow because I know that they consistently deliver valuable synthesised information in my interest areas.

- Trash/shred/recycle: after you have squeezed out enough of the juice from a source then get rid of it, it is of no use to you any more.

As a caveat, be prepared to reassess this on a regular basis, say annually. You may have achieved goals, require something new or discovered your real niche area.

Reflection

Use the tips for handling your professional reading. Address all the material you receive, either paper or electronic, and appraise its ability to meet your criteria for managing your career at the moment or changes you are making in your career. Use a journal or folder to record useful information such as events, people and industry direction. Does most of the material take up space on the shelves, or even lie unopened in your hall? Let's not think about those alert files we have popping up in our e-mail everyday. Start immediately by junking most of what you have lying around until you have worked out what and why you need certain information sources.

Work–life balance

Pick up any magazine, journal or newspaper and this concept seems to pop up. We are all talking about having it and wanting it – and it seems like a good idea but few of us master it. I think it is about the words themselves – work, life and balance. It suggests that we have 'work' and then we have 'life' and somehow we are trying to balance both of them. So here's the rub, is work not 'life' too? We spend a large part of our lives working. I was confused for a number of years and could not seem to get the dynamic right: one way for work and one for the other part (life). I could work effectively at one, but still be unhappy in the other. Why?

I started to think more about how the work and non-work parts of my life could be more aligned to what I want out of life generally: what inspires me, what is important to my relationships with family and friends and colleagues, money questions, my contribution, my vision and me. Once I started looking at all these areas my overall focus became clearer irrespective of whether it's about work or the other part of your life. If you have not read Chapter 3 ('It's all about you'), please do so as this will give you more details on how to marry the two together.

Using a journal

I have found this a very useful idea in order to shape my LIS career and it involves a spiral bound jotter. I use a regular A5 sized pad – you can use any size really but A5 is compact enough to carry around but big enough to write in. Feel free to replace it with a more technologically advanced tool if you are that way inclined! Each day I record items that I wish to remember for my development, such as names, events, information about niche sectors, examples of good practice, articles to read, further ideas for development, etc. Once a week I skim through and action some of the information, adding to my body of knowledge. Usually about 50 per cent of what I have written I score

Reflection and understanding for this chapter

This chapter expands our idea of managing your development as a LIS professional. I think the days are gone when we can solely focus on 'business as usual', with change being an everyday occurrence in the LIS sector. With that in mind, many of the ideas can easily be incorporated into your daily operational life as a practising LIS professional, and they will also help you to cope with change so you can reap the rewards in your longer-term goals and the targets for your career. The reflection points after each tip should be completed as you work through the chapter and will again help to raise questions in your mind rather than give an instruction to do so.

You should now have an understanding within yourself of the following ideas:

- accepting change;
- making a commitment;
- attitude;
- creative working;
- working outside your comfort zone;
- appreciation of what other industries can teach us;
- hard and soft thinking;
- being sociable and networking;
- planning to succeed;
- work–life balance;
- having a focused intention with professional reading.

through and take no further action. I have found it a very useful tool for my practice as a LIS professional for focus and development. I also use it to manage my everyday workflows.

Further reading

Heye, D. (2006) *Characteristics of the Successful Twenty-First Century Information Professional.* Oxford: Chandos.

6

Making the time for managing your career

After you have read this chapter you will be able to:

- understand why the principles of time management can help you take charge of your career;
- appreciate why you need to allocate time each day and week in order to take charge of your career;
- appreciate how your current career goals can be delivered more effectively;
- work out your 'real' commitment level;
- understand your relationship with time management and how that affects your ability to manage different priorities;
- understand the key performance indicators for good time management;
- understand that working on one thing at a time is a good thing to do;
- have a better understanding of dealing with everyday tasks and how to 'fit in' projects;
- understand that saying no can be the key to setting yourself free from time constraints;
- understand the importance of working on tasks every day;
- understand the importance of setting limits;
- understand why writing lists is not a good idea and how 'closed lists' will work better;
- identify and cope with randomness.

Introduction

Let me start this chapter with a whole series of questions. How would you describe your relationship with time? Do you think that time plays an important part in your quest to take charge of your career? What could you achieve if you were given more time? Just ponder these questions.

Let me ask you something else. Are you in a constant 'guddle'? Let me translate that for you. 'Guddle' is an old Scots word meaning a 'state of confusion or untidiness', and to me it is a perfect word (even the word sounds correct) to describe how we can feel about the apparent lack of time in our lives or our ability to control time.

You may be wondering why I have devoted such a large chapter to time management in a book about taking charge of your career as an information professional. The answer is quite simple. I believe that it is our perception and ability to manage and control time that can hold us back from either taking charge of our career or losing the momentum to realise goals in our career. Without a doubt taking charge of time is one of the most important things you can do to help manage your career.

The general principles of time management are an important tool in our quest to manage and take control of our careers. It is for this reason that some of our good ideas and resolutions about taking charge of our careers can fail. Whenever I have failed to reach a goal or keep the momentum going in my professional development it has usually been for reasons to do with mismanaging my time.

The sections in this chapter are not an attempt to oversimplify the various aspects we need to be concerned with in managing time. It is the examination and study of the application of good time management processes. It asks us as LIS professionals to address and review the processes and apply them in our careers. You will find yourself working not just more efficiently and effectively, but also freeing up time for personal development. Now ask yourself one further question: 'What can I use the extra time for?'

Who is managing your day?

Let's look at a typical scenario below and then consider the parts that are relevant to you.

> You decide it's a 'new year, new you' and you want to apply for the new systems librarian post in your academic library. Your workdays are busy, but you want to squeeze some part of your day into some concrete planning for how you are going to approach this job application.
>
> It is Monday, the first day back after the New Year break, and as you eat your breakfast you remember a couple of key tasks that need attention today. You have three ongoing library service related projects that require your attention today, one of which requires a presentation on Tuesday, one of which will be a short report on issues surrounding the document delivery system at the library team briefing on Wednesday and the last one you can't quite remember all the details but it requires a meeting on Friday morning. Today you are on the rota for the enquiry desk for an hour this morning (9–10 a.m. – your regular slot), but you now remember that you committed to cover for another staff member (for an hour this afternoon) as they have a dental appointment. You have a faculty meeting to attend today at another location at 10:30 a.m., where you agree to present a short paper on using Web 2.0

tools at one of their other meetings in two weeks' time. Although Web 2.0 is not 'your thing' no one else volunteered the time to prepare the short report and you don't like to say no to the faculty group.

During the day you need to go out and to pick up a birthday card and gift for your sister (her birthday is today) and a prescription for your regular medication from the pharmacist (you are on the brink of running out). Back to work, and eat lunch at your desk for five minutes while scanning through your e-mails. Some of these messages seem urgent and you are distracted into dealing with one particular item; this takes over an hour of your time. You will now need to take some work home as you have yet to attend to the items on your 'to do list'. A colleague contacts you to invite you to a meeting; they think your experience would be invaluable in helping facilitate their focus group. After a quick check in your diary the day seems blank, so you write them in. You continue to work on the three projects, skipping between each one in an effort to get ahead. A new junior member of staff drops by and asks for a 'quick tour' around the literature searching service and some training in using the biomedical databases; the three projects are discarded. You have distractions via e-mails and some telephone calls relating to a committee meeting you have to attend next week. You go home via the supermarket; you need bread and milk and you are out of cat food. You also pop by your sister's to hand in the birthday card and present. You are now in the house. You make the evening meal and stick some laundry in the washing machine. At 6 p.m. you eat your evening meal and deal with domestic issues relating to the family. It is 9 p.m. and you had planned to start an article for a library project you managed. You want to get it published but it's nearly 10 p.m. by the time you download your personal e-mails and some music from iTunes. From the work you have taken home you now realise that one of the items has a deadline for tomorrow's team meeting. You work until 11 p.m. and e-mail it to yourself. You had planned to research the competencies for the systems librarian post and work on some best practice examples. The article will have to wait too. You fall in to bed at 11:45 p.m. exhausted and stressed.

I will bet that some of the scenes from the above scenario will seem familiar to some of you. Let's hope not all at the one time. Everyone experiences varying degrees of time management issues – for some of you they will be perpetual and for others they are odd moments. Only you know what category you fall into. But let us consider again the above example. How did this person react to the situations around them? How did they work on the tasks that were not only a priority but at a crisis point (professionally and personally)? Did they say yes to people without thinking of the consequences, fail to prioritise their diary and readily give up time without proper consideration? So, based on the above scenario, at what point would they have had time to do anything apart from firefight at work and at home? The answer is none.

Your circumstances, both personally and professionally, will be different to mine – and indeed to anyone else's – and you need to identify what your situation is at this moment in time. However, I believe that there are some key common issues that can cause us to have time management issues. Do any of the following statements ring true for you?

- There are not enough hours in the day to get everything done.

- There is too much to do in one day.

- You feel that you are always rushing at the last minute to get work done.

- You feel that you have too many things to cope with.

- You find yourself involved in meetings that take up too much of your time and not everything is of concern to you.

- You always seem to be eating lunch on the go.

- You forget key dates and tasks.

- Coping with e-mail and other interruptions can be a problem.

- You are distracted by non-urgent tasks.

- You find it hard to prioritise urgent and non-urgent tasks.

- You are reactive in situations.

- You constantly firefight.

- You find it difficult to say no and put other people's wishes above your own.

- You get involved in and accept other people's inefficiencies.

- You have little time to relax and enjoy activities important to you personally.

- You want to spend time developing you career but can't find the time.

- You want more of a work–life balance but feel trapped in your situation.

The aim of this chapter is to demonstrate that the ability to manage time will be a major key to managing your career as effectively and efficiently as possible. In order to use time management principles we must first understand our own 'time management issues' and our ability to manage time generally. This will question our attitudes to time and our reaction to time issues. It will show that if we manage our time more efficiently and effectively, then we will do less firefighting and consequently be able to prioritise our personal and professional lives and so have a more creative and proactive role.

Let's get serious about time issues

Thinking about managing or controlling time can be quite overwhelming. After all, the notion of time has long been discussed in great depth in the sciences, the arts, philosophy and history, and this book will not attempt to comment further. However, suffice it to say, we cannot actually control time in any way, shape or form.

Most of us have uttered those words 'I need more time' or 'the day is too short'. But is it 'time' itself that is to blame? Let's remove the assumption that the technology for manipulating the fabric of time as in science fiction and many episodes of *Star Trek* is not yet available, so what do we do? We cannot 'get more time' by adding to the hours in the day and most of us have 'stuff' or commitments which we have (or want) to do daily that is not connected to our careers. So how can we get the best out of the day that is available without making us into miserable workaholics?

If we are serious about moving forward and taking charge of our careers, we need to take charge of time. To address the goals or issues of your career you will need to allocate time and energy, but where should that come from? I presume that most of you reading this book are working or studying or caring for a family and have many other items to deal with on a daily basis. As I have said at many points in this book, taking charge of our careers is not a single-track function. It is not possible to compartmentalise our lives into work and play, so let's work at bringing the two together.

I believe that I am quite a good time manager, but for the record I have had (and probably will have in the future) some bad time managed days. OK, so I have bad days, and with the best will in the world and planning that is unavoidable, but what I have learned over the years is to place the importance of completing work items in relation to each other and to manage them effectively. That is I work out the priority and order of tasks and complete them accordingly. Consequently, I have less crisis days of firefighting when I am just reacting to situations. With that in mind, there have been times where things have gone 'pear shaped' and I have failed to deliver for others and myself. When this has happened it has generally been the fault of bad time management by me at some level.

Let's get one thing right straight away. I don't believe that there is anyone who goes home at the end of the day thinking I have nothing left to do. The best outcome is always to have achieved the main activities and priorities of that today. I know that tomorrow I have a whole other list of things to do. But today I managed it – that, I think, is satisfaction.

Reflection: how do you use your time?

This reflective section asks you to understand how you use your time. Reflecting on what you have read so far complete the following example using Checklist 6.1 to log all events. This should give you an indication of how you manage time at the present.

- Consider a typical day for you personally and professionally – why not take tomorrow?
- Start logging from the moment you wake up until you go to bed.

(Cont'd)

- Make sure to log:
    - interruptions: phone, e-mail, favours, distractions;
    - planned events, activities;
    - forgotten items;
    - extra duties;
    - details you added to your diary;
    - what items you wanted to do but didn't get the chance.
- Take time at the end of the day and study Checklist 6.1. In a general sense study how you used your time and what you achieved.
- Who was controlling your time? You, other people and/or events?

Commitment versus interest

I believe that one of the main reasons that we fail to manage time has nothing to do with the 'concept or availability or manipulation' of time itself. It is a much broader question and is to do with our level of commitment.

Let's take this book as an example. This chapter – and indeed this book – will give you tools and ideas about how to best manage your career, but it is all completely useless unless you are willing to commit to putting them into practice or making this a priority in your life. I take it that by reading this book you have decided to take charge of your career and are interested in what this book can offer you, but without commitment it will be completely meaningless. This is a pity for you and me. This is a pity for you because you may never get to realise your own potential as a LIS professional and to put your plans and goals into action. And for me, because there is nothing more satisfying than when the work I have been involved in actually has a tangible outcome.

Checklist 6.1 How do you spend your time?

This process and using the checklist will help you audit how you actually spend your day at present. Start from the point you get up in the morning until you go to bed at night. Make sure you log:

- planned events, activities and tasks;
- interruptions (phone, e-mail, distractions, people);
- forgotten items;
- extra work taken on.

Just for the record I want to say that there is nothing wrong in being 'just interested' in things, whether it's drama, music, cinema, fitness, studying, cookery, whatever. But if you want some kind of success or tangible outcome from that interest then you will need a certain level of commitment.

As I know myself better than anyone, here is what I am interested in. I would love to run and complete a 10 km road race, and a couple of years ago both my partner and I talked about doing just that. However, come the end of the day or a Sunday morning I always seemed to have something else to do. On the other hand my partner was committed and we as a family were all at the finish line when he completed his first half marathon. Unfortunately my running shoes are still quite new after a few years. I am also interested in astronomy and was lucky enough to get a telescope from my partner a few years ago. I receive regular e-newsletters about astronomical events taking place over the skies of the UK and have all the information about the local university astronomy evening class I want to do. I do not feel disappointed at not having actioned any of these interests because I have achieved other things that have been more important to me over the last few years. But I am still interested in astronomy.

However, when I say that I am committed to having a work and personal life in balance, I mean it. Everything I do is related to what I believe is the best way to have a good life for my family and me. This includes having a fulfilling career for myself, which you will have read about in Chapter 3 ('It's all about you'). I also make concerted attempts to involve myself in projects and work that I feel matches my goals and allows me to have a personal life too. It is not just an interest of mine to make this happen, it is a real commitment. I work freelance, which people think must be great because you can organise your life in the way you want, for example get up when you want, watch morning TV, go for a swim when you want, meet friends in town – I can pick and choose when I work and how much I do. Perhaps you think it must be easier to have a good work–life balance if you work freelance? However, I also have a commitment to making money, paying bills, buying food and clothes, going on holidays, running a car, buying music, socialising with friends – and in order to do this I have to work and get paid. If I am working on projects and have to attend meetings or have deadlines, then going for a swim or meeting a friend for a coffee is not an option. If part of my goal is also to pick up my children from school and nursery, cook and have dinner with them every day then I need to fit my commitments around that. It means that work and personal development need to happen at times when I would be interested in other pursuits, so for the past four years I have worked nearly every Sunday and generally a couple of evenings during the week.

So here is the rub, when we think about 'commitment' we really need to face up to the word 'limits'. For some reason we seem averse to using the word 'limits', but the reality is that you can't do everything and limits can actually help in framing a plan to achieve goals. There is more about this later in this chapter.

When I started my training as a LIS professional I felt sure that my career path (and my skills) would be in the business information sector. However, on graduation I could not secure a job in the business sector – in fact 'I couldn't get arrested' as a LIS professional for some months after graduation. My first job was in health librarianship, something I had never even considered. But I remained committed to being involved in business information and two years after graduation I started work with a major consultancy group. Even although I was working in another area, I remained committed to my goal.

I was committed to writing this book in a certain time and because of that it has limited other parts of my life. However, during that year I was also committed to finishing a project on learning disabilities, presenting at a major UK conference, generating ideas for a new course, going on a family holiday for three weeks and completing an extension on my house. But actually one of the most important commitments was being able to pick my children up from school and kindergarten. My advice to anyone reading this book is to be committed to and focused on what you want for you and your personal and professional situation. If you need to reassess this then make sure that you have read and completed Chapter 2 ('Your LIS career I presume?') and Chapter 3 ('It's all about you').

Reflection

- Using Checklist 6.2 write down everything you are interested in or feel you are committed to regarding your career development and goals. For example, it could be a new job, promotion, writing for publication, networking, etc.
- Study each of your interests and prioritise in terms of interest or commitment.
- The next stage is to identify whether you are really working towards your commitments. Consider actions you are taking or priorities you set to make those goals come to fruition.

Do you know what you are aiming for? Writing it down

How do you make time for a goal or outcome when you are not 100 per cent clear about what you are aiming for? For

Checklist 6.2 Commitment versus interest

This reflective section and checklist is designed to help you audit your level of commitment to career goals. For each activity/task you must mark actions and plans you have underway in order to complete the goals; list each action separately. The final column asks you to register your level of commitment versus interest on a scale of 1–5. Level 5 shows a high commitment, Level 3 shows a level of commitment with perhaps a single action. Levels 1 and 2 highlight an interest level and show very little action. Level 1 would have no action at all. The outcome of this checklist is for you to see in black and white your real level of commitment.

Activity	Actions (list all)	Interest v. commitment (1–5)

example, say you are interested in working in a special library doing research and analysis work. Think about the areas that this could cover: the law, macroeconomic data on emerging markets, economic impact assessment, deprivation and poverty, housing market trends, oil and petrochemical markets, biotechnology, food industry. I could go on – this type of information work covers a huge and varied industry sector and sometimes requires unique skills and experience. Having some kind of clarity about what you want will help you remove obstacles in making time work better for you. If you have worked through Chapter 2 ('Your career I presume?') and Chapter 3 ('It's all about you'), then you will have a better handle on where you are coming from and where you want to go. This is not about having a 'mission statement' which can be general and slightly 'fuzzy' in nature – it's much more important than that. It should be absolutely clear as a bell, encompassing not only what you do want, but also what you don't want.

This book encourages you to practise writing things down. It encourages you to be specific about what you want and what you don't want for your LIS career. Use this book to help you, as it will free up time that you previously used on unrelated or non-specific tasks.

Getting things done, or just busy?

One of the things I hear again and again is, 'I am so busy with meetings, appointments, projects, etc. that I have no time for my own development and career goals.' But how much of this work is just being busy? Do you have to go to every meeting? Do you have to fill your day up with requests from others? Ask yourself this: are you busy doing work but know that you are letting other tasks fall by the wayside using the excuse that you are too busy to do anything else? If you find that you procrastinate about work then you will often use this excuse of not doing the work that really needs to be done.

The fact is that we are all busy. But does busyness actually help you achieve your goals and develop professionally and personally? No, busyness just means what it says – you are busy. The question we should be asking ourselves is, are we busy doing the right things?

I am making changes to this chapter and it is early in a new year. My diary and planner for this year is in front of me and there are lots of blank spaces. I already have some commitments filled in. But what will I be doing on the pages that are blank? Will I be sitting twiddling my thumbs wondering what to do, pensively waiting for the phone to ring and for people to give me work? I doubt that very much. No doubt I will have a full working day trying to fulfil my commitments to my work, career and private life.

Reflection

Look again at Checklist 6.1 and examine the log of all the events. Look to see if the tasks were examples of real work or 'just being busy' and whether they actually helped you work towards your goal.

Multitasking – multi-wasting?

At what point in the past did the term 'multitasking' become an acceptable process for getting things done? I have even seen on job descriptions the skill of multitasking to be included almost as a competency. Multitasking (as a verb or noun) has crept into our everyday vocabulary and I believe that it has led to confusion over ideas of 'volume' and 'quality'.

In case you have missed this idea completely, 'multitasking' is doing more than one task at the same time. There is also usually an element of performance associated with this. We all multitask – I can type this chapter and listen to the greatest hits of Madonna at the same time. However, I do find myself singing along to the words of 'Vogue' and perhaps, on occasion, trying to remember the dance that went along with it. So singing and dancing aside, not normally found in the LIS workplace, we could be distracted into doing more than one task. It could be writing a document while checking e-mails as they pop in, or dealing with requests from others, or trying to proofread a procedures manual. Unfortunately I have found (and there is research to suggest) that the analytical thought processes as well as work processes are affected by multitasking and can result in lack of attention to the main task in hand and perhaps even errors.

So while I am not in anyway blaming pop icons for affecting my personal performance, I know that concentrating on more than one thing is not effective. Have a look at your desk (workstation) right now. How many work items are open and are they all connected to the same task? This includes paperwork, e-mails, phone messages, research on Blackberries, etc., and is that Facebook open too? Are you skipping from one task to another?

So the message is, try and do one thing at a time. This seems perfectly reasonable. However, we live in a complex and fast-paced society driven by technology. Most of us have regular demands and vast information sent to us via the PC or the Blackberry. What about interruptions from e-mails and phone calls and realising that the meeting is in five minutes as our electronic planner bleeps into life?

The reality is that most of us have a large variety of work tasks on the go at any one time. There is the regular administrative stuff such as e-mails, post, making phone calls – aspects of our jobs that are repetitive (such as your monthly current awareness, your weekly teaching commitments, the weekly team meeting, processing the interlibrary loans daily). And then there are the more creative projects such as developing a new library service, changing the layout of the library, being a committee member of a regional or national group, working on or taking charge of your career.

Reflection

It is my experience that in order to achieve a myriad of types of tasks then we must try and dedicate our time and thought processes to one thing at a time. In practical terms what does that mean? Look again at Checklist 6.1 and consider whether you were trying to cover too many tasks at the one time. With hindsight, how could you have managed the day by working on only one thing at a time? How would you have organised it better?

Prioritise the important – first things first

Not all things are made equally important – we know this, right? So why in the middle of writing this chapter did I feel an overwhelming urge to check my e-mails? Firstly, it's a Sunday afternoon so very few clients will be contacting me with questions, and secondly this chapter is due very soon so it has more priority. I know exactly what is more important at this moment in time.

Let's say I follow my urge to check my e-mails. An alert list I developed for a client has been sent to me. I plan to work on that project tomorrow but decide that just for now I will see what is new in respiratory diseases for the learning disabled. Did that really take 15 minutes to check that e-mail? I don't believe that I am alone in this behaviour. So why do we find ourselves doing 'other things', knowing that ignoring a priority can be the start of a crisis situation? We know that procrastination or giving other tasks more importance due to pressure from others is never a good idea.

So how can we counter this effect? It is my experience that whatever projects or tasks are important to you or are required to be done by a certain time, you must do something on them every day. This is especially important if you know that you have a good lead-in to complete a job and we have all had those experiences when deadlines seem to stretch far and away into the distance and then suddenly, there you are out of time.

Reflection

Consider your activities for tomorrow. Write only what you will do and what you will not do, and include lunch, coffee breaks, etc. What tasks have priority over others? What will you do and not do? Here is my example:

- I will finish the preparation for the team brief on the new service level agreement.
- I will take time away from my desk to eat lunch.
- I will only look at e-mails in three batches tomorrow: first thing, before lunch and after 3 p.m.
- I will only work on the team brief service level agreement paper.
- I will start looking at my library project and see how I can get it published: 15 minutes in the morning looking at possible publications, 15 minutes in the afternoon drafting an e-mail to editors to ask if they would be interested in my ideas for an article and 30 minutes in the evening drafting out a framework for what the article may cover.

Now, using Checklist 6.3, work out what your aims are for tomorrow.

Checklist 6.3 What are you aiming for?

This section and checklist are designed for you to explicitly state what your aims are. Take your next working day and draft out the aims for the day. Include your regular working and continuing professional development for your career, or any other specific career goals you have.

Tasks (and associated time)

No is a very powerful and underused word

Why do we find it difficult to say no to some requests, especially when it comes to a work situation? It can be a minefield and often we fear that saying 'no' can have a negative impact on how people view us, especially if we say it to a senior colleague or to a boss. But what happens when we say 'yes' to everything? It can be a recipe for disaster. How can you possibly decide what really is important and set priorities for achieving results when you automatically say yes to everything?

This example was from a few years ago, but I think it illustrates a general position we may all find ourselves in. I was employed by a library services manager to do a project within a large library and within a short delivery period. Due to staff illness (it was the mid-winter flu season) the library was at one point severely understaffed and I was asked to help out at the enquiry desk. I was happy to help but only if the project deadline I was working on could be moved. The manager was adamant that the project could not fall behind as I could still work on it while at the enquiry desk. For anyone who has worked on an enquiry desk this can be quite a busy non-stop job, continually fielding questions and issues. I had to say no to their request. In the most calm and eloquent way I could, I pointed out that I would be rather busy on the enquiry desk dealing with the many users so the reality would be that I would have no time to do both. They were then left with the choice of what to do and what was most important to them. Ultimately, they found staff from elsewhere and my project finished on time. For the record, I was employed by this manager for another library project. They realised that I wasn't being difficult or awkward but that I had considered the situation and presented alternative scenarios to their own position – I was actually helping them reassess their own needs and goals. However, I was not providing any quick-fix solutions to their problems by adding to my own workload.

Sometimes we are sneakily taken in by the notion of doing someone a favour at work. LIS professionals I believe, pardon the generalisation, are very helpful people and work together well to get the job done. But there are some in the workplace who ask a lot of favours and perhaps do not reciprocate. In my early years as a LIS professional, the library team was asked to work on a backlog of shelving and filing. Each person, including the manager, was allotted a trolley of material to be done over a period of two weeks. I had just started my career in LIS work and a colleague, more senior to me, asked me twice to allocate some of my time to do her filing because she had organised meetings or training. By the third time she asked me to 'do her a favour' I knew what was coming. I was quite annoyed and felt that I was being taken advantage of. I reminded her that I had already 'done her a favour' twice, but in this circumstance I would have to speak to the manager as my own work was now beginning to suffer. I explained I was happy to help for the good of the team, but not to the detriment of meeting my own deadlines. I spoke to the manager and explained my concerns. A little later, I saw that person doing her own filing. If you are the type that does a favour on a regular basis, then reassess what you get back from others.

Saying no to someone is not an emotional or personal response, although it may initially feel like it. Be professional and counter your answer with the whole picture, your workload and the deadlines of whatever you are involved in. Don't be at the mercy of someone else's time issues – it's bad enough taking charge of your own. I doubt other people feel emotionally responsible for the extra work you have to take on.

Little and often

There are very few jobs that can be completed in one go. For example, it would be hard to write a library procedure in one go, develop a service level agreement, develop a training session and develop performance indicators for your library service. The 'little and often' principle helps to achieve quite a lot in small amounts of cumulative time. For example, say I am writing a new library service procedure. My first draft is really just a ramble of ideas, proposed headings and stuff that I want to expand on but don't know anything about just now. When I next work on the procedure I will expand some of the headings and perhaps do some research on the areas that are required. I may even contact and speak to people who have developed similar projects. I will continue to work on the principle of a few concentrated bursts of work and energy until it is completed.

I play the flute and have done for nearly thirty years. When I was young I played in orchestras and concert bands as well as having lessons. I would practise regularly, perhaps two/three short sessions per day and also play in the school orchestra another two or three times per week for two hours or so. These small segments all clocked up to a substantial amount of playing averaging 26 hours per week. Now take into account I was at school or university and had classes, had jobs, went out with friends, spent hours listening to music, read volumes of books and all the other stuff I did in my teens and twenties that is not publishable then it is quite a feat I managed to accomplish so much. Perhaps life was easier and more carefree then, but there were still only 24 hours in a day. As such, I reached quite a good level and became very proficient. I never disliked practising and it never seemed a chore. And all those little 30-minute sessions paid off.

So little and often will reap rewards. And you may find that your concentration will also improve. There is nothing so offputting as knowing that you have to spend a whole day working on the same task to get it done.

Even to this day I find it very hard to concentrate on anything for more than 50–60 minutes at a time so I split the day into concentrated bursts of time. Some I have no control over, like meetings, although I do try and limit my time in them. For meetings I always ask, what is my contribution to the meeting and do I have to go? I would recommend this principle if you find that procrastination could be a problem for you – and who hasn't suffered from that at some point? I believe that it is sometimes the sheer scale of a task (or its complexity) that can be offputting, so start by doing very small amounts of time (even 10–15 minutes) on projects to overcome procrastination and to start the ball rolling. All those little ten minutes will pay off.

Welcome to the world of limits

Do you have boundaries and limits in your LIS and personal life? Most of us (if not all of us) do. Limits can seem tiresome, but I believe that having limits actually helps us to achieve more. When a situation or a project seems very open and vague it is very hard to work on solutions. So if you are procrastinating about changes in your career because it seems like a huge task with endless options, then setting limits can help. You can read and learn more about limits in Chapter 7 ('Taking charge using project management as a tool') and Chapter 3 ('It's all about you') will help you understand more about your personal limits.

There are certain tasks that I need to do every day at particular times such as drop my children off at school and nursery and pick them up again. I may also have some after-school activities and then it's home to make and have dinner together. All this leaves me with very concentrated periods of time to work in, and at present I cannot change them. While that may be the situation I find myself in, most people really only have concentrated periods of time in which they can seriously work, and even if you work full-time you are not going to be fully effective for all 24 hours in the day. I am a more effective worker now that I have more limits and less time in my day compared to when I had less limits and more time. I use the limits to concentrate my work efforts and use the 'little and often principle' and priorities to make sure that work gets done.

Fear and loathing of lists

Up until a few years ago I was a 'classic' lists person. I loved them and used them all the time. I would merrily cross things off every day but also add a lot of other items to the list. These lists became 'Uber lists', sometimes of gargantuan proportions. It was hard to tell what I had achieved, but it was also perfectly clear what I had left to do. It was not a very satisfying process. However, a couple of years ago I came across Mark Forster's idea on closed (or 'must do') lists and dealing with backlogs (see the further reading at the end of the chapter). Hallelujah, I had found something that not only made sense but also actually worked. Over the years I have taken the idea of the closed list and moulded it into something that works for me, but the general rules are:

- You must be able to complete the list in one day.
- This is a 'must do' list and not a 'to do' list.

- You can choose the order in which you work through the list because you will always finish the list by the end of the day anyway.

- If you have a backlog of work create a backlog folder to isolate work.

- Batch similar work, e.g. e-mail, telephone, telephone calls.

- If new items crop up then do not action them until tomorrow and deal with them in batches.

Below is an example of my day using a closed list:

- Download all e-mail and scan through to allocate priority (15 minutes) (09:30 a.m.)

- Learning disabilities project (1 hour)

- Project work: draft article due in three weeks' time (30 minutes)

- Writing commission (1 hour)

- Project work: ongoing work for industry committee (20 minutes)

- Product review article (30 minutes)

- Lunch (30 minutes)

- Product review article (30 minutes)

- Project work: draft ideas for presentation in four weeks' time (30 minutes)

- Pick up children from school and nursery (30 minutes) (3 p.m.)

- Family time and domestic issues (3½ hours)

- Download all e-mail and scan through to allocate priority (15 minutes) (7 p.m.)

- Backlog work (30 minutes)

- Website changes and e-mail web editor with updates (30 minutes)
- Admin tasks (30 minutes)
- Tasks for tomorrow (15 minutes)

Reflection

Using Checklist 6.4, plan the next week using the 'closed list' system and in each day allocate time to your career development. You may copy and reuse this checklist as many times as necessary.

Random factors and understanding urgency

Do you suffer from randomness in your work? But have you ever considered who or what the random factor is? I am holding my hand up to sometimes being my own worst random factor. I see an e-mail drop in – who could that be and what could they want? A message from an online restaurant guide, new eateries opening in Glasgow – I suppose a five-minute look is OK. Someone sends you ideas on a training event, just a quick read through and a short reply ... who would know that it took 30 minutes of my time?

Do you recognise some of these random factors?

- You deal with e-mails as soon as they arrive.
- If you are on an electronic mailing list you read and answer most of the questions.
- You are distracted by a website recommendation (either work or non-work related).
- You immediately react to someone asking you to do work for them such as a boss or client.

Checklist 6.4 Closed or 'must do' list

This process should help you plan your day more effectively. Take your next working day, and using my example to guide you, plan the 'must do list'. You can re-use this as many times as you need – in fact you may find that you need to practise doing this on a regular basis to make it a habit. Remember you must complete everything on this list in one day, and with practice you will see what you are capable off. The little and often principle will also help you to stagger work.

Task	Time allocation (mins)

Most of us react immediately to random factors but the reality is that very few merit an immediate response. Do you find yourself always immediately responding to someone else? Some information jobs are organisationally designed for immediate responses such as enquiry deskwork. You may immediately respond to someone's request such as where and what are the passwords for accessing e-journals, but a request for training on biomedical database searching is not immediate. However, it is important and organisationally needs to be prioritised. If there are problems with this type of situation then it is an organisational problem, not time management. There should be procedures for dealing with types of enquiries such as:

- deal with immediately;
- same-day response;
- tomorrow or some other time.

Reflection and understanding of this chapter

You should now have a better understanding of your time management issues and how you can put into practice some useful tools for managing time in readiness for managing your career. Specifically you should understand:

- commitment versus interest;
- the effectiveness of working on one thing at a time;
- how to manage everyday operational work tasks;
- that working on tasks everyday helps to achieve goals;
- that having limits will help you achieve goals;
- the use of closed lists or a 'must do' list;
- how to deal with randomness: be it yourself, someone else or other things;
- that no is the best word that you know.

Further reading

Covey, S., Merrill, A.R. and Merrill, R.R. (1994) *First Things First: To Live, to Love, to Learn and to Leave a Legacy*. New York: Simon & Schuster.

Dodd, P. and Sundheim, D. (2005) *The 25 Best Time Management Tools and Techniques*. Chichester: Capstone.

Duncan, P. (2008) *The Time Management Memory Jogger: Create Time for the Life You Want*. Salem, MA: Goal/QPC.

Forster, M. (2000) *Get Everything Done and Still Have Time to Play*. London: Hodder & Stoughton.

Forster, M. (2006) *Do It Tomorrow and the Other Secrets of Time Management*. London: Hodder & Stoughton.

Forsyth, P. (2007) *Successful Time Management*, The Sunday Times Creating Success Series. London: Kogan Page.

Taking charge using project management as a tool

After you have read this chapter you will see the power that project management has in helping to deliver our LIS career goals. In particular you will understand:

- why project management principles and processes can be a useful tool to take charge of your career, especially scheduling;
- the importance of managing, delivering, controlling and evaluating projects;
- that the life cycle of projects will help you to initiate, plan, implement, communicate, evaluate and disseminate your career goals to give tangible results.

Introduction

This is a book about taking charge of your career. In order to do that more effectively there are some tools that I believe will help you to achieve your goals. In Chapter 6 ('Making the time for managing your career') we looked at how the management of time can help you take charge of your career by allowing you to work more effectively and efficiently. It is my belief that the principles and processes of project management are another tool that can help you manage your career. I believe that thinking about taking charge of your career as a project, or a series of projects depending of your goals, is a very efficient method.

This chapter utilises the processes of project management as tools to help you work out the most efficient and effective methods for incorporating your career wishes into your daily life. These tools, along with time management introduced in Chapter 6, will help you stay focused on where you want to go in your career and the steps you need to take to get there.

You do not need to have any prior knowledge or understanding of project management as I will explain all the fundamentals and show you how to apply these in managing your career. I have also tried to keep the language as simple as possible without using too many 'technical terms', but to aid you I have prepared a short glossary on the most common project management terms. This glossary may be found at the end of the book.

Why should I bother with project management?

I remember being at library school in the mid-1990s and one of the classes on the curriculum was 'Management', which included the subject project management. I was struck at the time at how this subject was being taught in such an abstract fashion. I could see that many in the class could not quite comprehend how they could ever use the processes of project management on a day-to-day basis in the library world. Some even questioned why learn about it at all? After all, are there not people who are trained as project managers?

However, I had a completely different perspective on project management. I had already used many of the principles of project management while working in another industry and had carried these through into my everyday life. There is a conception that project managers are already very organised people who know how things should be done, and by some 'genius mind' can work out what needs to happen, when, how much it will cost and when it will finish. This is untrue – everyone can learn the processes of project management and incorporate them into almost any aspect of their lives. Organising, managing and controlling the success of even very small projects requires much logistical thinking and planning. There can be too many variables and permutations so that having some kind of methodology is useful. So, even if you consider yourself to be disorganised, the principles of project management can help you.

The true power of project management processes is that they are a methodology for managing some kind of 'change process'. What could be more of a 'change process' than managing and taking charge of your career? The real secret is that it is the principles and processes of project management that allow you to visualise and control tasks in the way that is most efficient and effective to achieve your desired outcomes. In easyspeak, project management is a tool that helps you get to where you want to go when you want to be there.

This chapter considers the principles, fundamentals and processes of project management and shows you how you can use them in helping you to take charge of your career. You can also use this to help with any other aspects of planning change in your personal or professional life. However, I do recommend further reading for those of you that find yourself more heavily immersed in large projects and require further information, especially on the risk analysis and financial sides. You will find a selection of extensive project management resources in the further reading at the end of the chapter. These resources will give more detailed advice on change control, scheduling processes, managing risk and controlling costs. If you find that project management becomes 'your thing' then consider becoming certified as a project manager through the Association of Project Managers or the Prince Methodology programme.

So what about the argument that project management can only be used for certain project types? How can you take project management and use it for your own needs? The short answer is that from my experience I know that using these techniques will work and I have used them professionally and personally for over twenty years with success. I have used them as a planning engineer in the construction industry, and I have taken these same skills and re-used them for moving into the LIS sector. I have also used them for managing my career development from public sector librarian to private sector information worker and finally to independent information professional. The principles work and they will work for you.

Project management ... what's it really about?

Everyone uses the principles of project management in everyday life, whether you know it or not. Consider this common scenario. You are required to go to a meeting first thing on a Monday morning. The meeting is in town at 9:30 a.m. at a library you have never been in before. You will be attending the meeting, but will also be presenting the feedback from a recent training day you managed on behalf of your own library. These are some of the items you may have to consider:

- You must be there on time, preferably 5–10 minutes early. This is a non-changeable milestone.

- You have to decide on your mode of transport: bus, train, car or long walk. With each of these modes there comes issues and risks that can affect your ability to arrive on time.

- You need to consider transport issues and risks: the bus stops outside the meeting venue, car parking is limited and costly in town, the train is more leisurely but requires a walk at the other end, there are many entrances to this library and you are not sure where the meeting is being held in relation to entrances.

- Other issues: you need to drop your children at school first, but school doesn't start till 8:50 a.m.

- Milestones: the meeting starts at 09:30 a.m., you are on the agenda to speak at 10:10 a.m., you need to be back in the library by 12:30 p.m. to cover your slot at the enquiry desk.

- Your presentation needs to be completed by the Friday before the meeting as you are enjoying a birthday weekend break and will not return until 10 p.m. Sunday night.

- You need to leave work by 5 p.m. on Friday afternoon as your flight for the birthday weekend leaves at 7:30 p.m.

- The chairman of the meeting requests that all presentations are sent to them by 6 p.m. on Friday evening to be loaded onto their system to ensure flow of information and continuity.

I could go on, but I am sure that most of you will recognise this generalised situation. Our lives are very rarely easy to manage, especially combining our needs as a private individual and our career wants. Most of us believe that 'time' is the real issue stopping us achieving our career desires. I hope that Chapter 6 ('Making the time for managing your career') has now shown you how we can use time management to our benefit. Project management will also help you with the management and control of your time, but it is most effective in identifying tasks and scheduling events to realise our career goals.

I trained in the construction industry as a planning engineer where the principles of project management are heavily engrained into your psyche. I also worked as a site engineer involved in the day-to-day operational 'how to build' work, which includes working out the exact positioning for the building structure and also quantifying materials such as 'how much concrete do we need for a lift shaft?' Real 'nitty-gritty' stuff. So fundamentally it is about 'how do we do something and achieve a goal when change is involved?' Does it seem so far-fetched to then say let's use project management to help us take charge of our careers?

When project management is taught, as in my case at library school and also when I studied engineering, it is reduced to a very abstract subject. It is usually about inanimate objects like buildings, services, procedures, etc. I have yet to hear any tutor talk about it in any other format, so it is of little surprise that students see little relevance for the principles elsewhere. Even if you pick up a book on project management it is usually geared towards major projects and the more mathematical side of project management. Don't get bogged down in what constitutes a project in the LIS sector but it could be such things as though not limited to:

- marketing a new service;
- bringing two services together;
- writing procedures for a new database;

- physically building a new library;
- moving a library;
- digitising a collection and developing a new taxonomy;
- reworking an existing service.

It is my experience that the underlying methodology and processes can be used as a tool just as successfully for you as a professional. I have used project management as a tool for:

- managing my career when entering the LIS profession;
- identifying ways in which I could move from one LIS sector to another;
- managing my re-entry into the workplace after a career break;
- continuing professional development;
- writing a book;
- marketing my services.

Now you don't need to have trained in the construction industry to know that you need foundations before you build walls and that you cannot put a roof on without a supporting structure. Similarly, you can't take your career forward if you haven't worked out your personal constitution (see Chapter 3 'It's all about you'), audited where you are in your career and decided what you would like to do next. So read Chapter 3 if you haven't already.

The next fundamental then has to do with the method by (or order in) which you choose to do tasks, i.e. the steps that you have identified you must take to get to where you want to be. One mistake that people constantly make when talking about project managing is that there must be 'only one correct way' to complete a project. The most important thing that you must remember is that usually there is no perfect (or correct) way to complete tasks or projects, there is only a selection of more or less efficient and effective methods of completing tasks. Think of it as a map of how to get somewhere, on which there is usually many different ways of getting to a destination.

However, in saying that, sometimes there are some tasks that have to be done in a certain way or order. When we are working, usually there are associated resources (people and/or materials) that will be required to complete the work, so that may set some limits (see Chapter 6 'Making the time for managing your career' for more about limits). There may also be financial considerations. For taking charge of our careers, what resources will we require? Will there be any financial implications such as further training and travelling to events? Consider also whether we need people to help us along the way – a mentor, your line manager, or your professional association.

At its most basic level this is what project management is all about: a methodology for managing change and innovation. I think that sounds like a valuable tool in taking charge of your career.

Managing, controlling and delivering?

Let me start by saying that there are many brilliant books and useful methodologies on project management. However, it can be quite a 'dry subject' to inject a little bit of excitement into. If you have ever tried to read a project management book – and I have read many in my career in the LIS sector and as a planning engineer – then you will know what I mean. But to be fair, if you become heavily involved in project planning and monitoring the time durations, financial costings and risk analysis for projects then you need to read more beyond this chapter.

But relax, it's not all rocket science. Essentially it's a plan of how to do and manage a series of tasks (known as the schedule), and how to deliver to budget and to scope. As usual there is a 'but'. The 'but' here is that it will require some hard thinking on your part. These are some of the questions or ideas that project management can help you with:

- Encapsulate what you are trying to achieve in the fullest possible way.

- Work out a method or order for completing the tasks in an efficient and effective manner.

- Consider whether there is a certain time frame.

- What people will be involved?

- Do you need any other resources?

- Will there be any associated costings?

- Are there any associated risks with these tasks?

- Are there any underlying issues?

- What happens if some unexpected events happen? What effects will they have on the project?

- Will everybody understand what is going on, including yourself?

- Who do you have to interact with or who will be affected by the change?

- How will you know that the project is successful?

So if you have a series of tasks (or a project) and you can work through the questions above then you will be well on your way to making change happen for you. Do not underestimate the power or importance of these questions. You need to be able to work through them in order to make things happen for you. If you skim over the basics of what you are trying to achieve then you will have a plan that will almost be meaningless. I believe that some people want to be 'doing things' and be busy. However, imagine your disappointment when you realise that your busyness may result in nothing. This is also especially true when things do not go to plan (as will generally happen), and there is no plan to fall back on.

Have a start, a middle and an end

The good news is that project management tools focus around life cycles of projects, and this is an excellent way for us to focus on making changes to our careers in an efficient and more controlled fashion. After all, we want to be able to start a project, have a middle bit and then finish. Personally, I think we all need a 'personal ticker tape parade' as we congratulate ourselves in completing projects.

So here is the life cycle in project management:

- Initiate and define: what is the project about and are there any constraints?
- Risks and issues: what is happening or may happen that will affect the project?
- Plan, schedule and control documents: research, time questions and logical methods.
- Implement: monitor and track.
- Evaluate and review: successful outcome or not at appropriate stages, e.g. start, middle and end?
- Communicate: report progress.
- Disseminating phase: who needs to know about this?
- Measuring success and success criteria.

It is also excellent news that we can use each of these life cycle phases to motivate ourselves and realise our career goals. By working through these processes we will also develop documentation that is needed to support our goals. The documentation I have produced in the past has had official names such as scoping reports, specifications, budgets, etc. and will record key decisions, assumptions and the methodology of what it is I am trying to do and what I expect as an outcome. But don't be a slave to 'officialdom' – your paperwork will be just as important if you give it names such as the following:

- This is what I am trying to do.
- This is how I am going to do it.
- This is how long I have to do it in.
- This is the order I will be completing the tasks in.
- This is how much money I need.
- These are the people I need help from.
- This is how often I will check up on my progress.
- This is the record of how successful this project was and the lessons I learned.
- This is the outcome of the project.
- This is the article I wrote on 'How I managed to return to work after a career break'.

Stage 1: Initiate and define

Who wants to do this project and what are they trying to achieve? As it is our careers then we are the ones initiating the project and we will also be defining what our goals are. I have developed a checklist to help structure this process

135

(see Checklist A.1 in the appendix at the end of the book – this may be copied and re-used as many times as necessary to help you define your ideas). Checklist 7.1 provides a completed example of my own to help you.

Generally the structure of initiating and defining falls into six key areas, as follows:

1. What must this project achieve?

2. What are the project objectives?

3. What is the scope of the project?

4. What is the timescale of the project?

5. Are there any milestones (key dates) associated with the project duration?

6. What resources do you need to do this project?

Stage 1: Reflection

Reflect on what you have read so far and my own personal example.

- Consider one small project in your career you wish to manage.
- Use Checklist A.1 from the appendix at the end of the book to work out:
  - what the project must achieve;
  - what the project objectives are;
  - what the scope of the project should be;
  - any milestones;
  - the timescale;
  - any resources.

You may copy and re-use Checklist A.1 as often as you wish.

Checklist 7.1 Initiate and define the project: example

Here is an example from my own professional development where I used the initiate and define process.

What must this project achieve?

- To improve my writing skills as an exercise in continuing professional development.
- To promote my work as an independent information professional.
- To increase my profile nationally, as an information professional, on a variety of LIS subjects and showcase my talents as a freelance worker.

Project objectives

- Have articles published in three national trade press.

Scope of project

- Identify key areas of my work that I want to showcase
- Identify some key publications that I would like my work published in
- Get advice on how to approach editors and the type of work they publish
- Identify editors and contact them
- Narrow down article ideas and approach editors
- Write copy

Timescale

- 4 months

(Cont'd)

Milestones

- Start June – must finish end of September
- Holiday September for 1 week
- Start new client project 1 October

Resources

- No financial costs
- Extra time required – work evenings and weekend

Stage 2: Risks, issues and constraints

There is a difference between risks and issues. Risks are things that may affect the project and you may not or may not be aware of them. Issues are already in place (they may be happening) and you are aware of them. For example, you have family commitments, it is the start of the academic term, there are more teaching commitments for the library service and you have volunteered for a professional association committee. You can take issues into account when you start the project. Constraints which you already know about should also be taken into account. For example, you have no spare cash for formal training courses so plans cannot include this, or you have committed to volunteering time at a youth group one evening a week so this cuts down the time you have available.

Risk management will involve identifying potential risks and estimating probability and impact. This is a major aspect of managing projects and some people are highly specialised in estimating and controlling risk situations. If you are involved in major project management situations within your work environment it is essential that you read further and perhaps take examinations in this specialised area. However, it is fair to say that analysing risk can generally be a very subjective area and will be dependent on your own personal nature. Some of us are risk-takers and some are more risk-averse. I would say that I am a more of a risk-taker so I am generally less pessimistic about outcomes and the scenario not going to plan. However, I do rely on a detailed plan of work to help me organise and realise my goals, so when things go wrong (which they tend to do as I do live in the real world) I know that I will always have my plan to fall back on and get me back on track. If you find that you are more risk-averse or know that you are more pessimistic in nature it may be worth using a mentor to help you through this process and put risk into perspective. For our purposes risks can be classified as high, medium or low level and are related to the possible impact.

I have developed a further checklist to help manage these points (see Checklist A.2 in the appendix at the end of the book – this may be copied and re-used as many times as necessary). Checklist 7.2 below provides a completed example of my own.

Checklist 7.2 Record risks and issues: example

This example follows on from Checklist 7.1 and my endeavours at writing for publication and general marketing of my business.

Task	Risk/issue/constraint	Action
■ Contact editors ■ Develop ideas ■ Write article ■ Holiday	■ Summer time: people on holiday ■ Lack of interest ■ Editor not interested ■ Takes longer than anticipated ■ Flight home has been changed to next day	■ Contact more publications ■ Research other publications ■ Factor extra evening work ■ Factor weekend work

---

> ## Stage 2: Reflection
>
> - Reflecting on what you have read so far and my own personal examples of risks and issues, reconsider your own project from Stage 1.
> - This time revisit and, using Checklist A.2 from the appendix at the end of the book, list all the risks, issues and actions you may need to take.
> - You may copy and re-use Checklist A.2 from the appendix as many times as you need.

Stage 3: Planning and scheduling the project

This part of the process may require some research either internally or externally. For example, external factors that may affect projects could be political, procedural or social. It is also useful to understand good practice, so ask around for advice and seek out people who have had similar experiences or are particularly knowledgeable in specific areas. You will probably have your own network of friends and colleagues, but reach out more widely through electronic means to get a better, more honest response to your requests. Discussion lists can be especially useful. I particularly like Freepint (*http://www.freepint.com*) – it is free and the variety of information is quite astounding. The Chartered Institute of Library and Information professionals (CILIP: *http://www.cilip.co.uk/*), American Library Association (ALA: *http://www.ala.com*) and Association of Independent Information Professionals (AIIP: *http://www.aiip.com/*) all require membership to access discussion lists. It is worth noting that some of these groups have Facebook pages that are generally open access.

One of the most important documents and processes in project management is the project schedule. This document identifies all the tasks, each task duration, any relationships that individual tasks have with each other (interdependencies), any milestones (or critical dates) and – importantly – the overall duration. This document can be a very detailed programme and will depend on how complex your project is. In very straightforward terms the schedule breaks down your work plan into manageable pieces of work with attached realistic time frames. Time can be calculated in any unit you wish – hours, days, weeks, etc. I tend to use hours or days for small projects associated with my career development as I am slotting in these activities where I can. Estimating the duration of tasks can be tricky, but be realistic, not overly optimistic, and always identify when you can't work.

With scheduling you must also consider when you will do work. If you work a 9–5 job then it is highly unlikely that you will come home and work straight through on a task that has been allocated eight hours. Personally, if I am involved in development work, I like to schedule in two hours per evening. I generally never work on Saturdays but do work on Sunday afternoons for four hours. I never work late into the evening as I am not at my best after 9:30 p.m. This works for my own personal circumstances. Only you will know what works for you and your situation – perhaps a quick read through Chapter 6 ('Making the time for managing your career') will help you.

I have developed a checklist to help structure the tasks and work out the sub-tasks within a project (see Checklist A.3 in the appendix at the end of the book – this may be copied and re-used as many times as necessary). In very simple terms the sub-tasks are the step-by-step tasks you have to do in order to complete the main task. You can also record your estimated durations. Checklist 7.3 shows a completed example of my own.

Checklist 7.3 Record tasks and estimate time durations: example

We will follow on from the last example and break down the scope to identify tasks and establish estimated time durations. Estimating the duration of tasks can be tricky, but this will get easier the more you practise.

Main task 1	Time estimate (hours)
Identify key areas of my work that I want to showcase	3 hours

Sub-tasks

Go through recent projects
Think about what people would want to know about me

Main task 2	
Identify some key publications	2 hours

Sub-tasks

What do I regularly read?
What are my peers reading?
Where do I think my work would be most suited?

Main task 3	
Approach editors to confirm the type of articles they are looking to publish	4 hours

Sub-tasks

Contact editors I already know
Contact people I know that have been published
Identify people who are well known
and where they are published

(Cont'd)

Main task 4

Identify editors and contact them   1 hour

Sub-tasks

Compose e-mail outlining ideas
I have for publication
Ask them if they have any special
issues coming up

Main task 5

Write copy

Sub-tasks

What does a freelance information
professional actually do?   8 hours
Mental health inequalities project:
how did I plan and manage this
project?   8 hours
Searching tips for non-English
language health resources   4 hours

To work out the overall duration you need to add up all the estimated durations. In this example the total time is estimated to be 30 hours.

Stage 4: Scheduling and control

Although a key phase of scheduling is to allocate time to your tasks you need also to know in what order you can do the tasks. Ask yourself whether any tasks need to be completed before others can begin, and whether some tasks are dependent on others being finished first. Interdependency (or logic) is important, but working out overall duration is also important.

The next phase in the scheduling process calls into use mathematical logic diagrams. You may have heard of some of these processes before – they will be called something like:

- critical path analysis;

- precedence diagrams;

- logic diagrams;

- PERT analysis;

- GANTT charts.

These allow you to work out the overall duration, what activities are critical to the completion of the project, whether you have any 'slack time' (sometimes called float) and whether are there any activities that are relationally linked together. There are three ways in which you can schedule:

- Pencil and paper – old fashioned, but quick and easy for small personal projects.

- Proprietary desktop applications – examples that I have used and are common are:
  - Artemis
  - Microsoft Project.

- Open-sourced web-based applications – useful free applications are:
  - Project.net
  - Project Pier.

If you become involved in managing a large project then I would suggest you make the case for purchasing one of the proprietary desktop applications. However, the open-sourced web-based versions are great for managing small personal projects. Microsoft Project is also a good standard and covers many personal and professional applications.

One of the key features of using the schedule is that it will identify your critical path. In its simplest term that will be the series of tasks that are all interdependently linked and which if they are not completed on time will cause the project not to meet the finish deadline.

For more simple projects and my career development I tend to schedule using an action plan. I have developed a final checklist to structure the schedule (see Checklist A.4 in the appendix at the end of the book – this may be copied and re-used as many times as necessary). This shows the task, who is responsible, start dates and finish dates. Checklist 7.4 shows a completed example of my own.

Stage 4: Reflection

- Reflecting on what you have read so far and my own personal example on planning and scheduling, let's reconsider your own project from Stage 1.
- This time revisit and use Checklists A.3 and A.4 from the appendix to list all the tasks and durations.
- You may copy and re-use Checklist A.2 from the appendix as many times as you need.

Stage 5: Implementation phase

This is a fancy way of saying 'actually doing the project'. It is the monitoring and tracking phase, and this is what gives project management the element of control when trying to achieve certain outcomes in a generally uncertain environment (i.e. everyday life). It is important in any implementation that there is some form of reporting on progress. Reporting back procedures are imperative to the

Checklist 7.4 Action plan: example

Again this follows on from the example I have been using throughout.

Task	Responsibility	Start date	End date	Time estimate (hours)	Overall duration
Main task 1					
Identify key areas of my work that I want to showcase				(3 hours)	
Sub-tasks					
Go through recent projects					
Think about what people would want to know about me					
Main task 2					
Identify some key publications				(2 hours)	
Sub-tasks					
What do I regularly read?					
What are my peers reading?					
Where do I think my work would be most suited?					
Main task 3					
Approach editors to confirm the type of articles they are looking to publish				(4 hours)	

Task		Time
Sub-tasks		
Contact editors I already know		
Contact people I know that have been published		
Identify people who are well known and where they are published		
Main task 4		
Identify editors and contact them		(1 hour)
Sub-tasks		
Compose e-mail outlining ideas I have for publication		
Ask them if they have any special issues coming up		
Main task 5		
Write copy		
Sub-tasks		
What does a freelance information professional actually do?		(8 hours)
Mental health inequalities project: how did I plan and manage this project?		(8 hours)
Searching tips for non-English language health resources		(4 hours)

success of any plan, so mark up weekly where you are and any problems that have occurred that may cause slippage in time. Also record how you remedied situations. This can also be an excellent way to record any financial details and for continuous improvement when doing similar projects.

Implementation example

Here is a further example from my plans to get into publishing. I had arranged to meet with someone who publishes on a regular basis who was going to give me an insight into leads for editors and possible journals worth considering. They have cancelled at the last minute – annoying, but it does happen. What do you do? I consulted with the Action Plan and here are some of things that I considered in order to keep the momentum going on the overall project.:

- Immediately ask them to suggest possible dates for reschedule.
- If they are unavailable full stop then identify other people.
- Go with the information you have at the moment.
- Use up slack time you have available in the plan to wait for another meeting or use it to find someone else.
- Review the project and reduce the scope to perhaps only try for two publications.
- Work harder and assign more hours to the project, but still finish on time.
- Accept that the project is slipping and there will be a new end date – last possible suggestion.

Stage 5: Reflection

You can do this two ways. First, keep to the example you have been working on throughout this chapter and implement it. Or second, start afresh with a new 'real-life' project, use all the checklists provided and then implement the project.

Stage 6: Communicating and reporting

Who will you report to on your progress, how are you doing against your success criteria and do you have to take any action? If like me you are an independent worker then I report to myself. However, I try to involve other people, like mentors, in my development and I use them to report to on what I am doing. Most of you will have co-workers or colleagues to which you can communicate your plan, and I firmly believe you will have a higher success rate if you communicate and report on progress to someone. However, this is your career and you are taking charge so you decide. Be absolutely honest about this and don't be tempted to cover up your lack of progress. One of the reasons could be that you are setting yourself unrealistic targets. If, however, you have a mentor or someone to bounce ideas off then reporting to them on a regular basis will hopefully keep you on the straight and narrow and perhaps you will understand where you may be going wrong.

Stage 6: Reflection

You can do this two ways. Firstly keep to the example you have been working on throughout this chapter and implement it. Or start afresh with a new 'real-life' project, using all the checklists provided.

149

Stage 7: Project completion, evaluation and dissemination

Once you are nearing the end of the project you must identify how the project has worked out. What did you actually manage to achieve? You must be able to 'close off' projects. Having a reporting mechanism is also useful and if you have a mentor or another colleague you may want to summarise what the main outcomes of the project were.

Completion, evaluation and dissemination example

For the publishing example I decided to close off the project by writing another article based on how I kick-started my own professional development (which included writing articles) over a four-month project. The article is detailed in the resources section at the end of the chapter.

However, the article covered information on the general evaluation of any project and included:

- Did the project achieve its outcomes?
- Did the project have any unexpected outcomes?
- Did the project stay within time and budget?
- Did I learn anything new from the project?
- Would I do anything differently the next time?

Evaluating and disseminating the project outcome is invaluable to having closure. It is important to remember that not all that you set out to achieve may have happened. In fact the process may have opened up other areas that you had not considered before.

Stage 7: Reflection

You can do this in two ways. First, keep to the example you have been working on throughout this chapter and implement it. Or second, start afresh with a new 'real-life' project, using all the checklists provided. Consider the completion of your career project: how did you evaluate it and disseminate the work?

Reflection and understanding for the chapter

- You should understand and be able to use the principles and processes of project management including:
  - identifying objectives and outcomes;
  - considering resources and finances;
  - considering risks and issues;
  - working out tasks and time periods;
  - considering milestones and critical time periods;
  - working out an action plan;
  - working out whether there are any financial implications;
  - closing the project with an evaluation;
  - disseminating the results.
- In this way, you will have used the principles and stages of project management to take charge of your career.

Further reading and resources

Allan, B. (2004) *Project Management: Tools and Techniques for Today's ILS Professional*. London: Facet.

Association for Project Management (2006) *APM Body of Knowledge*, 5th edn. High Wycombe: APM Publishing.

Barker, S. and Cole, R. (2007) *Brilliant Project Management: What the Best Project Managers Know, Say and Do*. Harlow: Prentice Hall.

McCarthy, R.C. (2007) *Managing Your Library Construction Project: A Step-by-Step Guide*. Chicago: ALA Editions.

Nokes, S. and Kelly, S. (2007) *The Definitive Guide to Project Management: The Fast Track to Getting the Job Done on Time and Budget*. Harlow: Financial Times/Prentice Hall.

Project Management Institute (2004) *Guide to the Project Management Body of Knowledge (PMBOK Guide)*. PMI.

Ptolomey, J. (2006) 'A 4-month plan: organise and plan for personal and business development as a freelance information professional', *JINFO Newsletter*, 132, 16 November. Available online at: *http://www.jinfo.com/newsletter/*.

Useful websites on project management

American Society for the Advancement of Project Management: *http://www.asapm.org/*

Association of Project Managers: *http://www.apm.org.uk/*

Australian Institute of Project Management: *http://www.aipm.com.au*

International Project Management Association: *http://www.ipma.ch/*

Project Management Institute: *http://www.pmi.org/*

Project management software

Artemis: *http://www.aisc.com/*

Gantt project: *http://ganttproject.biz/*

Microsoft Office: *http://office.microsoft.com/en-us/project/*

Project.Net: *http://www.project.net/*

ProjectPier: *http://www.projectpier.org/*

International project management standards

APM Body of Knowledge: *http://www.apm.org.uk/*

PRINCE2 Methodology: *http://www.prince2.org.uk/*

Part 3
Different stages of your career

8

Career breaks

> After you have read this chapter you will understand how to manage breaks in your LIS career. Specifically this chapter discusses:
>
> - that taking career breaks is not something to hide;
> - the guises that career breaks can come in;
> - the issues surrounding career breaks;
> - steps to re-enter the LIS workforce after a career break.

Introduction

I follow a column in a professional library journal called *Information Scotland*[1] written by two 'youngish' recent librarian postgraduates – I hope they don't mind that reference. As I was writing this chapter their most recent column considered the career break – or as they called it, 'explaining the blind spots'. They further defined the idea by considering them as periods of time not spent working in your chosen career, i.e. the library and information sector. I thought this was a very interesting and honest article, as having career breaks, 'blind spots' or gaps as an information professional is usually something that we try to smooth over.

It is, however, a common problem I believe for many people in the LIS industry and there are many possible reasons we as information professionals have these 'blind spots'. When I think back to my postgraduate course probably around 50 per cent of the people on the course (including me) had worked in another industry before. Around 20 per cent of the people had come straight off a first degree, usually unrelated, and the remaining 30 per cent had some kind of job in a library (usually non-professional grade) or were unemployed. There is a good chance that most of the people from my cohort had 'blind spots' or career breaks. There is a good chance that some of you reading this book will also have had career breaks, and from reading recent reports about people entering the LIS industry this still seems to be a problem.

If you have read any other general books on managing your career, then you will know that employers may be suspicious of people who have these 'blind spots' in their career history. Specifically, I believe that what most employers are suspicious of is unexplained career breaks. This chapter is about taking the guesswork and uncertainty associated with the career break out of the equation for the employer and for you as a LIS professional. It is my experience that career breaks and explaining them (as you will have to) are not such a major issue. In fact I have had three breaks, each for different reasons.

This chapter is very important for anyone working or about to start working in the LIS sector, because I believe that we should be upfront about the fact that career breaks are a fact of life. By glossing over difficult (or unexplained) situations you may indeed be glossing over some very important features in your own life. If you have not already picked up on the general idea of this book then let me just explain it one more time. The way you want to live your life, the things that happen in your life, your motivation for working in the LIS sector, the work you choose to do as an information professional and how you manage this all together is what keeps us happy.

Should I be daring to include a chapter such as this in a LIS career book? This is a serious issue for the sector and we should be questioning as an industry how we can attract people (very probably from other industries) and help people flow back into the sector after a break (as employers tell me all the time how expensive it is to get people with experience). Let me just say for the record, I have been honest about my career ups and downs and difficulties in librarianship and I am absolutely fine. This has included not only how I managed to move on from career breaks when I entered the industry, but also when I took time out to have a family. In recent years I have read more and more articles in the professional journals about the problems of entering or re-entering the LIS workforce so there does seem to be some issues associated with doing so.

This chapter therefore offers some practical tips and guidance on managing a career break and the steps to take when re-entering the work force (or for first timers starting out in the industry).

What can give rise to a career break?

There are obviously quite different reasons why people take career breaks – personally I have had one career break before entering librarianship and two since. My first break came in my late twenties just before I started on the route into librarianship. Essentially my lack of motivation to stay in the construction industry combined with the terminal illness of a family member gave way to 18 months of nothing much apart from worry and much sadness. To put it starkly, it was a very difficult period of my life. After working in the LIS sector for quite a few years I had two happier career breaks with the birth of my daughters.

There is a whole range of reasons why a career break can occur. Firstly, you may decide that you wish to engineer a break to do other things (like a sabbatical) or to break a particular cycle (your current career/job no longer excites you or you find yourself in a difficult personal situation). Secondly, this break can be forced on you, e.g. as a result of downsizing or reorganisation – otherwise known as losing your job. Thirdly, there can be the reorganisation of your personal life through something like parenthood as mother nature engineers your break. I had not long started as an independent librarian before I discovered I was pregnant for the first time – it was such a surprise I did not tell anyone for a long time. And finally, career breaks can also come sweeping in out of the blue, for example through illness, of yourself or of someone close to you, or through catastrophic events like the death of someone close.

The formal career break: the sabbatical

This is perhaps the most straightforward break to have and also to explain to future employers. You can use a sabbatical to travel (this is probably the most common reason), to study, to learn to play a musical instrument better – in fact anything you want. I have known a couple of LIS professionals to take sabbaticals for six months to travel and they both returned to their original jobs. Having a sabbatical sounds like a brilliant idea – time away from work with your job being held open for you. If you work in a large national organisation they may already have a formal policy for dealing with requests for sabbaticals. But I also know of a smaller local organisation that was also able to cope with this situation.

The most important question that you need to consider when applying for a sabbatical is your reason behind having a career break. Do you really need a career break or you are just fed up with your current situation? You must remember that you will be asking your employer for quite a lot of understanding coupled with financial and administrative reorganisation on their part so do them the courtesy of giving this idea a lot of thought. Heye (2006) pointed out that you really do need to think your ideas through before you approach your line or human resources manager – you are essentially trying to sell the idea to them. Contrary to popular belief employers want to keep staff, as it is an expensive process to recruit and train new staff. A well-informed employer with a reasoned brief by an employee on taking a career break, perhaps indicating the benefits to them as an employer, could do the trick. As with everything, honestly really is the best policy. So, why are you looking for time away from your job and employer, how much time do you need, and do you have goals for your time away?

The essential point to bear in mind is that you are asking for an employer to keep your job open, so it is only right that you think through the proposal from their point of view as well. If the real reason for a sabbatical is that you feel that you can no longer work (or don't want to) for an employer then be truthful about this. Employers can be soured by employees that fail to return after a break – they feel slightly cheated as they have gone out of their way to keep your job open and made practical and financial arrangements for temporary staff. Remember, you will also need a reference from your most recent employer when you do eventually move on. So, don't confuse taking a career break with just being fed up with an employer.

Use Checklist 8.1 to help you work through your ideas for taking a formal career break and presenting the idea to your boss or line manager.

Checklist 8.1 The formal career break (sabbatical) planner

Use this sheet to help you formulate your reasons for taking a sabbatical.

Why do you want to take a career break?

Career development ☐

Travel ☐

Family time ☐

Learn a new skill ☐

What else? _____

How much time do you need?

1 month ☐

3 months ☐

6 months ☐

More than 6 months ☐

Do you intend to come back to your job?

_____

Taking into account the fact that you will need money, are you sure you want to return to this employer?

_____

Do you have any goals while away on sabbatical?

_____

_____

What can you bring to your job after a sabbatical? New skills, ideas, renewed energy?

_____

_____

What makes this a win–win situation for you and your employer? What is in it for them?

_____

_____

It is also important that you find the right time to approach your employer. Do not ask for a quick five minutes to discuss the idea. Ask your line manager for a scheduled meeting to discuss your development and then carefully discuss your thought processes and ideas. Show your employer due consideration by allowing them time to consider your plan and what they could offer you. However, an employer is within their right to refuse your request so you should consider what your options will be if this is the outcome.

The unforeseen career break

An unforeseen career break may be the result when life stops you in your tracks. There are many reasons for taking time away from work – ill health (physical and mental), changes in your relationships, family problems a traumatic event such as death or injury, or some other singular event in time. First of all, you are entitled to feel what you feel so sometimes it is better not to 'soldier on' but to take some time out. It does not fall within the remit of this book, but perhaps you may need to seek the help of a professional to be able to cope with some of the changes that you are facing or have faced. When you decide that you are ready to return to the LIS sector use this book as a tool for auditing your skills and experience and for focusing your efforts in order to meet your personal success criteria and goals.

Other types of career break

Things that fall into this category are more usual occurrences such as parenthood (and I include men in this too). I know someone who has three children (six, four and six months) and wants to be a 'stay at home mum' until they are all in school. She has calculated that at that point she will have been away from the library workforce for ten years. She has already noted the stellar changes in the industry landscape since the birth of her first child over six years ago and has concerns about her ability to find work and reintegrate back into the workforce.

Issues around career breaks

However sound your reasoning was for having a career break, when you decide to actively re-enter the LIS workforce you may find that you have more questions than answers and knowing where to start can be a problem. You may have concerns specifically around the following:

- Confidence – or the lack of?
- Skills – are they still useful, relevant?
- Industry landscape – changes in the LIS industry, especially over the last ten years, mean that some jobs don't exist any more in their old format, and what about the new job titles that don't mention librarian or information?
- Gaps – and how do you explain them in your job application?
- Circumstances – you may have a different attitude to what you want from a job and may want to downsize work or indeed start escalating work commitments.

Re-entering the workforce may make you feel like you are starting from the beginning again and you have nothing to gauge yourself against.

Getting back to work

Starting with you

This whole book starts with the question of you and finding out what you are about and your personal and professional circumstances. If you haven't already read Chapters 2 ('Your LIS career I presume?') and 3 ('It's all about you'), then go back and work through the reflective processes and checklists to find out more about yourself. You may feel that while your skills and experience were acquired a few years ago and although technology may have changed, basic essential information management skills are still as relevant.

Now that you are more in tune with what you want and don't want, what interests you, and where your skills and experiences lie, you are in a better position to think about moving forward. Into the bargain, you can explain to potential employers that you have methodically worked through where you want to be in your LIS career, what skills you have and what you have to offer – this will show a commitment and enthusiasm for your industry and your personal development. Employers can't help but be impressed by someone who takes control and manages their career in this way.

Work experience

Probably one of the most valuable things you can do for yourself if you want to ease your way back into the industry or cannot find the job you would like is to get work experience. This could be voluntary (no payment) or contract/agency work (paid but not regular employment).

Voluntary work experience

I did voluntary work in the LIS sector after I achieved my postgraduate degree. I know many other LIS professionals who have also done this to gain experience and confidence. Let's be up front about it: it is far from ideal not getting paid to do work but consider the alternative. No experience, no job, no money ... the worst possible combination. Without experience I had little hope of getting a start elsewhere so I volunteered at a medical library for a few months after finishing my postgraduate qualification before getting a paid job. This paid dividends a couple of years later when I went to work in the private sector: they cited my commitment and ethics to working as a LIS professional with my volunteer work and it was this level of making things happen for myself that got me the job.

This is probably one of the easiest things you can do to start the ball rolling again. Not only will you get credible work experience, you can start practising your skills again and learning some new ones (without the big step of becoming a full employee). Don't forget the psychological effect of working and being with people again – it can start to have quite significant effects on your whole well-being and outlook on life, and you can't download that on a social networking site. Into the bargain you will then have a referee for any job you may apply for. Here are some things that you can do or think about:

- Work out the sectors that interest you the most and you would like to work in and get paid by (eventually), e.g. health, public, voluntary, business. Make a short list of organisations you could approach.

- All different types of libraries and information services are looking for volunteers as they generally are short staffed and have smaller budgets. So think about a local public library, hospital library or voluntary sector information services if you are thinking about re-entering the workforce in a small way at first.

Agency/contract work experience

This type of work experience is a step further up the ladder from voluntary in that you will actually get paid for what you do. Again when I started out in the industry and couldn't get a 'professional librarian's job for toffee', this was the easiest way to stay focused, get experience and make some money. If there is one sure thing about the LIS sector it is the sheer variety of work we can find our professional skills a requirement for. It is an excellent way to try out different LIS sectors and types of work they offer. It also helps you decide whether you love or hate a particular sector – you may dream that media librarianship is for you but the sheer pace of the media sector may leave you gasping for breath. It is also a great way to network and meet lots of different people in the industry – they will have an influence on you and perhaps provide guidance and advice on how you could more forward, particularly if you find yourself working in a sector you absolutely love.

Many of the professional associations offer their own recruitment and agency services, so if you are a member make them your first call. There are also specialist recruitment agencies for the LIS sector. As a start, make sure you read any of the monthly industry magazines – they all carry ads for the recruitment companies.

Professional associations and sector groups

Professional associations and voluntary sector groups can be a great way to help you re-enter the workforce. So even if you are on a career break, keep up your professional association or niche industrial sector membership, as you will have access to industry news, networking events, low-cost training sessions and the chance to participate in groups and committees. Usually these associations and groups will have a heavily discounted unemployed rate, so it is worth taking advantage of this. I am a personal member of Scottish Health Information Network (£7.50 per year, at the time of going to press), and for that I get access to a closed message list, low-cost training events and a professional journal. But I also get to participate in working groups and committees. While I was keeping a low profile with babies I spent a couple of years involved in the journal editorial group and continuing professional development group before becoming involved in the main committee. It is my experience that you get the chance to relearn skills, learn new skills and keep up to date with your niche sector or interests, and get an opportunity to network.

There is no doubt in my mind that my involvement in a niche LIS industry sector group has paid dividends many times over. Being involved in this organisation has kept me connected to the industry when I did not have the time, or to be honest the inclination and energy, to focus on my career. When I did want to re-energise my career I used the organisation to repackage some of my skills, sharpen up old skills and learn new skills – and I even made a few new friends.

Reflection and understanding for the chapter

- Consider some of the issues around career breaks or 'blind spots'.

- Consider whether you want to take a formal career break from your employer and how you can sell the idea.

- If you have taken a career break, have you worked out what you now want from a LIS job – if not then go back to Chapters 2 ('Your LIS career I presume?') and 3 ('It's all about you') and rediscover yourself.

- If you are looking to return to work in the near future, then start planning on how you will do it – will you target sectors, have you reassessed your skills, how can you update skills (through voluntary or contract work) and how have you been keeping things ticking over?

Note

1. Fallis, R. and Ross, T. Information Scotland: *http://www.slainte .org.uk/publications/serials/infoscot/contents.html*

Reference

Heye, D. (2006) *Characteristics of the Successful Twenty-First Century Information Professional.* Oxford: Chandos.

9

Starting out, making it count

At the end of this chapter you will understand:

- the importance of understanding the library and information landscape;
- the different ways in which you can gain experience and get the most from short-term, low-paid or even voluntary work;
- what you feel interests you or is important to you and the skills you have to offer;
- how to take responsibility for your career;
- what to do when you have identified a specific job or sector;
- how to increase your competencies or skill sets outside your job;
- how to manage your professional development.

Introduction

I started out in the library and information sector over twelve years ago on a postgraduate course and I had already been involved in another industrial sector for ten years before that. The year before the course started I had been trying to get a library job – that elusive first job! – and it was very frustrating. Furthermore, on completion of the postgraduate course I naively thought that employers would be waiting to snap me up.

Almost immediately on completion of the course the bitter wind of the reality of job hunting and the sparseness of jobs really began to sink in. To put it bluntly I couldn't get arrested as a librarian when I graduated. This was a complete shock to me – I had ten years of actual work experience (albeit in another sector), and I was genuinely interested and excited about working in the library sector. I was as enthusiastic as a mosquito on a hot balmy night. The evidence was that people with library experience were consistently getting jobs over me. To get a paid permanent contract in an area/sector that you find worthwhile is challenging and it is a serious 'chicken and egg' situation for the new professionals.

I have read two articles recently that have reminded me that many librarian graduates encounter similar problems today and have 'generally had a few years of doing other things' before embarking on a career in this sector so there is always the element of catch-up. If you fall into this category it may be useful to read Chapter 8 ('Career breaks') if you haven't done so already. It seems that in the last twelve years it has not changed that much. If you read through many of the industry trade magazines or professional association journals or meet newly qualified professionals via work or at conferences then it seems just as hard today to get experience and get that first proper professional job.

So what can you do when you start out in the industry and there seems to be limited jobs on offer? How do you get that all important experience and real professional job?

This book, as I have stated in the introduction, is not about 'how to get a job'. This would be a promise I could not possibly honour. But what is important about this book is that if it used for enquiry and as a guiding tool it should prepare you for taking charge of your career in your first tentative years in the LIS industry.

If you have not already worked it out, I want you to take responsibility for what it is you want from your library and information career – no one else can take this responsibility for you. I am asking you to be genuinely excited and interested for your career as a library and information professional. If you cannot then don't expect things to flow your way. It is that simple. This book will provide you with the tools and techniques to help you question the whys and suggest how you may craft your career, and although this chapter is dedicated to newish or prospective professionals there are other chapters of the book that are equally useful too. I will draw your attention to these as we go through the chapter.

Understanding your industry

Without a doubt whatever level you are starting at in the industry you need to have a full picture of what the industry landscape looks like. If you have not already read through Chapter 4, please do so now as this will fill you in. I speak from experience in this matter as someone who did not (at the start) have a real grasp of the industry when I considered it as a career – a cardinal sin, but isn't hindsight a wonderful thing? Back then the industry did seem to be more straightforward and job titles simpler to understand.

You will also need to get to grips with the different modes of work you can do such as:

- traditional library and information roles;
- non-traditional library and information roles;
- independent work.

If you are just starting out in the industry I very much doubt that you will be going down the independent route at first, but if you are thinking about it for the future then read Chapter 11 to build up your skills set.

The professional associations have a role to play in educating you on this aspect of the industry and you will find their websites useful in identifying job types, salary scales and qualifications required.

One of the major changes in the industry since I entered it is the sheer volume and variety of work in which you can find yourself involved. So if your reason for entering the profession was to find a quiet backwater to issue books (and yes I have heard that from someone recently), then prepare to be shocked by what you can do and how you can make a difference.

Reflection

Make sure that you have read through Chapter 4 ('Check out the view – the LIS landscape') and understand the scope and size of the LIS industry. Now identify one of the major broadsheet newspapers (appropriate to where you live or want to work) that have jobs listings, ideally on the day when they have all types of sector jobs listed. Work your way through them and identify the jobs that could potentially fall into the LIS market.

The buck stops with you

It does not matter whether you are just starting out in your LIS career or have been in the industry twenty years, there are specific questions that you will have about taking charge of your career. You need to address these questions specifically, so if you have not then please work your way through Chapter 2 ('Your LIS career I presume?'). Furthermore, you need to be aware of what is important in your life, reflect on what you have done up to this point, and consider your skills and what you have to offer.

Chapter 3 ('It's all about you') deals with this in detail, so you must complete this also before you can move forward.

Both of these tools are for guidance in self-awareness and self-knowledge. They are designed to help you focus on starting out and moving forward into the library and information services sector. If you start out with fuzzy ideas of what you want from a career as a LIS professional then you need to expect that your journey will be fuzzy and undefined.

If you find that you are starting in the library and information sector and have had experience elsewhere or have had some career breaks, then you will need to address these issues. Chapter 8 ('Career breaks') discusses in more detail the issues around career breaks or 'blind spots' or 'gaps', or just time spent doing other things.

Although this book is not about how to get a job, an employer could not help but be impressed by a person who undertook their career with such an enquiring and methodological approach. Use your work undertaken in this book to help focus your ideas and thoughts for any job applications or interviews you receive.

Getting experience

There seems to be no doubt about it, you need to be able to get experience in the industry as soon as possible. Having library and information service experience is your passport to ultimately getting the job you want. When you are starting out in the industry it is very possible that you accept that there may not be the availability of the type of experience that you would like. The remit of this book does not permit investigation into why there is a dearth of opportunities for people starting out in the industry, but instead asks you to consider how you can generate the best situation for yourself. Chapter 8 ('Career breaks') discusses some ideas for getting experience, so re-read that chapter to refamiliarise yourself.

From my own experience the situation has not much changed since I entered the LIS workforce over a decade ago when I had never even considered health librarianship as a possible option for me. However, that was the job that first presented itself to me. An eight-week part-time low pay grade library assistant post. To be honest, it hardly sounded like the golden ticket.

However, first impressions apart, it was the start of my interesting road into library land. When thinking about taking on this type of work there are many factors to consider and they can all help to tick some personal and professional boxes for you.

- If you have no experience, then any experience is a bonus.

- If you have no income, then any income is a bonus.

- It is for a short period of time, so if the job is turns out to be less desirable than first thought then you are not tied to it.

- If you work hard for the eight-week period and nothing materialises then at least you will have a LIS professional who can give you a professional reference.

- It is likely that on a low pay grade then you will be doing a lot of 'donkey work', but it will be everyday operational library work and you can get a feel for what goes on in a library service.

- Even if most of your job involves a photocopier and/or time shelving the stacks then work out what skills and responsibilities you have acquired. Businesses – yes library services are businesses – operate because all tasks are completed, with the administrative work usually being a very important piece of the jigsaw.

- While you are working, enquire about other work opportunities – and that includes volunteering some of your time if there is no money for other paid employment.

- Volunteer a couple of hours per week to learn to catalogue or help in the document delivery service. That would be another two skill areas and shows willingness to learn.

- Trade your time for learning a specific skill. For example, a very good skill to have is the ability to do literature searches – this crosses a multitude of sectors such as biomedical, business, finance, legal and academic. Give some free time in exchange for someone teaching you how to use one of the large fee-based databases.

- If you enjoy the sector you are working in, enquire what competencies and skills they require of professionals in their team. Ask if you can shadow a staff member for a day to get a broader understanding.

- Use your contacts wisely in the eight weeks. Ask your boss if they know of any other short-term work options or other professionals that need some help.

- When you leave stay in touch and ask for consideration for any jobs that come up.

The idea when you are starting out in the LIS sector is to get as much out of any experience you are given. Be proactive in looking for work, spread yourself across the industry and use all available networks to find out about work:

- the university department you graduated from;
- Freepint network job listings: *http://www.freepint.com/*;
- library and information professional association recruitment agencies;
- recruitment agencies particularly for the LIS sector;

- local press and national broadsheets;
- library and information professional associations and industry publications.

When you have a clear idea of what you want to do

It is possible that you will have very definite ideas of what sector you want to work in and possibly the type of job you would like. This is great news, but also comes with a warning. I have seen many a new entrant into the library sector disappointed by their lack of progress in, say, getting a post in the media sector or as a systems librarian. I had very clear ideas about working in the business sector, but it took me two years to secure a job as an information professional for a consulting group. In the meantime I concentrated on building up my generic skills as an information worker. Keep your focus, but don't close off your ideas to other work that you had not considered. To finish off the story, I spent a few years in the business sector before returning to the health sector. It turned out I enjoyed health more than business in the end, so remember those eight-week low-paid contracts could eventually pay dividends.

If you are keen on a particular sector or job then you can start turning your attention to building specific experience and skills competencies. You will need to start researching the sector – try using the following tips to build up your understanding.

- Research the sector or job speciality you are most interested in.
- What competencies or skill sets are required for this?

- Follow the industry news and start pulling together information about your particular interest.

- Identify organisations and perhaps people who interest you.

- If certain people interest you then start to research material they have published.

- Contact people directly in your chosen field and ask them for some time. Show your interest in their area and explain how you have been preparing yourself. My experience is that generally in the LIS sector people are prepared to help others and will give up time.

- If you are in a niche sector (special library group) such as law, business, health, chemical, etc. then seek out professional organisations or voluntary organisations and people that represent this area. You will find that many of the library and information professional associations have specialist groups that are free to join for students and unemployed people or low cost for people on low incomes. Joining these groups will immediately increase your knowledge of the sector and make networking and other opportunities more easily available.

When you are looking to increase your skill set and competencies outside your current job

It is very possible that even when you have your first professional job in the LIS sector that there will be limitations in the skills and competencies that you can build up. It may not be possible to get involved in special library projects to develop yourself. The good news is that there are plenty of opportunities to build up skill sets outside your normal job structure. One of the most straightforward routes is via your professional association or specialist industry library group. There are always opportunities for committee and group work and you will get the chance to manage and deliver projects, be involved in committee work and help to manage and deliver training events. One way to broaden your horizons, and especially if you are looking to move into another sector, is to develop and network with contacts in another sector. Furthermore, think like an information professional and use your competitive intelligence to your benefit. Research potential organisations and the types of services they operate.

You should also consider more solo efforts such as writing for publication and speaking at events and conferences to raise your profile.

Managing your professional development

There is no real difference between managing your professional development in the LIS sector when you are starting out in the industry and when you are more senior in the industry. I would, however, draw your attention to Chapter 5 ('Tips for keeping up with business as usual and managing change') so that you begin to think about how you can make some small changes in your daily life that will have big impacts in managing your career.

Keeping up to date in the LIS profession can be difficult and time-consuming. As part of our jobs as information professionals we help our users or customers avoid the pitfalls of information overload. We must endeavour to do the same for ourselves. Also, part of our professional development must surely be about our responsibilities and the attitude with which we action our commitments.

Chapter 5 reaffirms how we should approach our careers generally and the way in which the following can help:

- embracing change;
- attitude;
- creativity;
- working outside your comfort zone;
- best practice from inside and outside the LIS industry;
- different ways to think;
- networking;
- planning and goal-setting;
- work–life balance;
- professional reading;
- having a journal.

Making the most of the electronic world

As library and information professionals we operate in an electronic world for much of our time. We very often will find ourselves as teachers of this electronic information world as part of our everyday work. Use these skills to keep tabs on the LIS sector through:

- e-discussion lists and newsletters;
- blogs;
- professional portals;
- social networking sites.

I have included a list below of some you may find useful to start with, but as you make your way in the industry you will find more for yourself and fellow professionals that interest you by what they have to say.

Reflection and understanding for the chapter

This chapter should have given you a better understanding of:

- the library and information landscape;
- the different ways in which you can gain experience and get the most from short-term, low-paid or even voluntary work;
- what you feel interests you or is important to you and the skills you have to offer;
- why taking responsibility for your career is one of the most important things you can do;
- what to do when you have identified a specific job or sector;
- increasing your competencies or skill sets outside your job;
- managing your professional development.

Further reading and resources

Freepint: *http://www.freepint.com* – UK-based library and information professional portal. Sign up to get the Freepint e-journal, which will give you an insight into other sectors and people you should be aware of. Their other publication *FUMSI* (*Find, Use, Manage and Store Information*) is also excellent. Sign up to access the Freepint bar, a useful discussion forum for professionals at all levels.

Jinfo: *http://www.jinfo.com* – from the UK-based Freepint (*http://www.freepint.com*) group, a clearinghouse for jobs. You can also sign up for their newsletter.

Lis.jobs.com – a useful US website for discussion, newsletters and blogs. *Info Career Trends* is a very useful newsletter, even if you are not US based. Developed and maintained by Rachel Singer Gordon.

10

Managing and leading

After you have read this chapter you will be able to:

- question whether you are ready to move up to the next level;
- understand the difference between leadership and management;
- see whether you are drawn to leadership or management;
- understand the key ideas of being a manager and the skills you need;
- think like a leader;
- understand why your personality type matters;
- understand more about the behaviour and traits of managers and leaders;
- understand how to get the necessary skills as a leader or a manager.

Introduction

This chapter seeks to provide coverage on the ideas of leading and managing people, and investigates the skills we may require as leaders and managers in the LIS industry. This chapter does not provide an extensive coverage of all ideas about leadership and management – for that we would need a whole book to do it justice. This chapter concerns itself with how we can take practical steps to move our careers into managing and leading people and teams. There are some very good texts available that provide more extensive background and theory and I have provided some useful extra reading at the end of the chapter.

What do you think of when management and leadership are talked about? Are you reminded of Dilbert, the US comic strip that satirises the micromanagement of the office workplace and organisational culture? Or could it be the television show *The Office*, another parody of mismanagement and leadership? There are many that may think I am poking fun in this chapter and perhaps not taking it too seriously. On the contrary, I believe that both of these satirical views of leaders and managers provide useful insights into some of the skills we require as managers and leaders. It is easy to see via the Dilbert cartoons or *The Office* TV series when management and leadership situations seem ridiculous. On the other hand, when you have worked with a good manager or leader it's hard to put your finger on what makes them so good and why the situation seems to work. The question for you then is how do you know what skills you need to gather?

If you are reading this chapter on the understanding that you are ready for management and leadership then there are a few golden points that you need to remember. Firstly, up until this point, you have been judged by your own ability to do a good job; when you move into a management or leadership role you will be judged by your ability to get your team to succeed. You are now highly dependent on your team for success. Secondly, your staff (or team) will always reflect certain behaviour ... yours. Therefore if you want your staff to behave in a certain way, then behave that way yourself. Always remember the shadow that you cast.

In the first couple of paragraphs of this chapter I have used the terms managing and leading together. However, they are very different beasts requiring different skills sets and can be played out in different scenarios. Let us consider the following statements:

- Leadership can be an aspect of being a manager but managers may not always be leaders.

- You can be appointed a manager or apply for a job as a manager but you become a leader.

- You don't need to be a manager to be a leader. A leader can inspire you and others to achieve great things and show you the path for delivering goals, but they need not be the manager.

- You can be a leader in your field but you may not necessarily have the operational skills to run a service or a department.

Reflection

Stop for a moment and think about some of the leaders and managers that you know. Do some of the above statements relate to them?

This chapter is not about what leadership or management is, it's about what you can do to expand your capability to manage or lead. Although this chapter does not provide extensive theory and background, there is an enquiry into understanding more about the differences and influences of leadership versus management.

Are you ready for the next level?

After a few years in the LIS industry, building up experience and competencies as an information professional, we all start to question whether it is time to move up to the next level. The question of being 'time served' comes to most of us; we have spent our days learning the ropes in the stacks, at the photocopier, etc. By virtue of time should we not be ready for moving up into management and leadership? The answer to this question depends on how you have been spending your time: have you been doing more or less the same job for quite a few years or have you been taking on progressively more responsibility and more complex projects? If you want to start moving into leading and managing you need to be taking the responsibility to show that you are ready and have been developing the skills necessary.

Leadership versus management

As I mentioned briefly in the introduction to this chapter, there is some confusion around the differences between managing and leading. In fact, I have sometimes heard them used with the same meaning. We must consider the focus and influence of these two roles and what makes them distinctive in their own right.

Firstly, let us consider the manager. Managers are usually internally focused on the operational procedures and problem-solving. For example, they may be responsible for the day-to-day running of a library, its service and its staff, or if the service offering is larger then perhaps a particular aspect of the service such as document delivery, e-services or information literacy. Secondly, let us look at the leader. Leaders are usually externally focused and create vision and strategy for the future development and role of the service; they use influence to work towards goals. For example, you may have realised a few years ago the importance of Web 2.0 tools for your users and worked to implement them in the operational running of your library and information service.

There is no question that one is better or worse than the other – just remember that managers and leaders have different roles to fulfil and are important to the success of any business. Good managers are equally as important as good leaders. You can be both, or either.

There is, however, a caveat to the differing roles of the manager and the leader. The manager, although interested in day-to-day, business-as-usual, operational processes and procedures, should also have some leadership qualities. A library service, just like any other business service, should be developed and delivered with key success criteria and measurement of the benefits (or impact) at the heart of its delivery processes. Therefore a good manager will be constantly tweaking operational processes and procedures for accountability, performance and value.

Reflection

Reconsider the basic ideas surrounding leadership versus management. Next look at some task you are involved in at the moment and work out whether it is focused towards either management or leadership. You can use Checklist 10.1 to note down your ideas. Generally do you find yourself involved (or naturally gravitate towards) management and/or leadership?

Next recall where you feel your main strengths, skills and wishes are – remember Chapter 2 ('Your LIS career I presume?') and Chapter 3 ('It's all about you') will help you work this out. Ask yourself: 'Is there a stronger focus on or desire for either management or leadership?' For example, are you more interested in the internal focus of the operational running of a service or do you have a low boredom threshold for the day-to-day? Would you feel more connected to the outward focus of leading a service development or project?

Finally, consider the organisation you work in at the moment and its level of bureaucracy and politics. Does it consider leadership and management only to be appropriate at a senior level or does it allow for development at various levels within its structure?

This enquiry into your current situation, along with your career wishes and skills, should help you decide whether your goals can be satisfied in your current employment. If not it may be time to think about where you can best exploit your talents and interests.

Checklist 10.1 Managing or leading?

(You can copy and re-use this checklist as many times as necessary.)

Summary of work

Management

Leadership

Management

What do you need to be thinking about and what skills are required as you move into managing or management in the LIS sector?

Start at the end, not at the beginning

This whole book encourages you to think about where you are now and where you want to be at the end of your journey, and then provides the checklists and tools to get you there. It is the same when designing and managing a LIS service: consider the success factors/criteria or performance indicators that will need to be reported and how you will measure or realise the success or benefits of the service. To put this into easy-speak and paraphrase the likes of Covey (2004), start with the end in mind. What are you trying to achieve? For example, when running a literature search service, how many people using the service would be considered a success? Does the service seek to provide a value-added element to a particular 'high kudos' group of users so that you can measure directly the impact in terms of 'new business'? Or does the service provided support ongoing consultancy work, so that you can accurately show where the information service supports client work?

Working out what needs to be done

Generally this concerns itself with processes and procedures in order to deliver a service. How will the service run? What do we need to do to run a service? How will it work? What order should things be done in and what paperwork do we need? This simplifies the priorities and ensures that everyone knows how to perform a job and the standard that is required. It also helps to identify obstacles and remove them. It should be an example of effective usage of time and resources, in that it should be the big picture but seek to remove replication of work done elsewhere to streamline a process.

How about resources?

We must also consider the element of resources, be they people, money or equipment, that are required to deliver a particular service. For example, what staff (professional and administrative) are required to deliver a service level agreed community-based health information service? How much will it cost (direct overheads, equipment, travel, etc.) and how many computers and location hires will we need?

It does not matter what sector the library or information service is in, these are the main criteria that a LIS manager must be considering.

Management and the skills I need

There are many different definitions of management, and I could fill this whole chapter with analysing and synthesising them. You should read some of the other texts, listed at the end of the chapter, if you want to debate the finer points of the definition of managing. However, they all essentially boil down to a couple of fundamental ideas. Managers make the best use of resources, plan, motivate, process, facilitate, monitor, measure success, set standards and outputs, budget finances and goals, and deliver results.

There are also two golden rules that you must always keep in mind. They are short and to the point and are centred on people.

1. *Managing your team* – know what makes up a good team and how to use it to your advantage. If you are not familiar with Belbin's (2003) team roles then I would urge you to get to know them.

2. *Managing yourself* – know that how you manage yourself will be reflected onto your team and will show in their respect for you and ultimately their work output.

Reflection

Identify a project (or a piece of work, or an aspect of the service) that could help to build and showcase your management skills. Ask to be responsible for this and then use these tips to help manage it.

1. Start with the end goal – what are the success criteria?
2. Work out what needs to be done. If this is on ongoing service then you may need to audit it first of all.
3. What resources are required?
4. Think carefully about the skills you need and how you will deploy them.
5. At the end of this project examine how you managed the process. What do you need to be working on, what skills are you weak on, how could you have better managed a situation?
6. Remember, you will not be perfect. This is all a learning experience.

Leadership

Who wants to be the leader?

Is there a crisis in new leaders coming through in the library and information sector? Some believe that there is and it seems linked to the rapid and exponential changes in libraries and the convergence of information management and IT, with reports that we are seeing interlopers in our patch. If that were so this would be another book completely, so I will leave you with your own thoughts in this area. I believe that whenever there are periods of transformation and change then it is the perfect opportunity to make a difference via leadership. I believe that leadership is both a noun and a verb, a name or badge, but also a call to step up to the mark and show action. The ability to accept, embrace and work with change is an important prerequisite for being a leader. The chances are that if you don't really like (or embrace change) then leadership is not for you.

This chapter hopes to encourage some action research on the information professional's part by asking you to enquire what you can add to this debate. What are the real skills that leaders in libraries require? Where are the examples of best practice? How can I add to innovation and creativity for my profession? Remember you do not need to be a manager to be a leader.

Transformational or transactional?

The LIS sector has and is undergoing transformational changes and growth which, depending on how you view the situation, is either an opportunity or a threat to the profession. Bryson (2006) suggests that this calls for a different type of leader in the LIS profession to cope with the larger and more complex issues. It is called transformational leadership and includes being 'proactive, visionary, entrepreneurial and risk-taking'. It relies on building a shared sense of the goals to be realised by all the team. It is a more charismatic leadership style and sets out to provide a space in which innovation and inspiration are encouraged from all team players irrespective of their level. That means that everyone in the team has a say and creative thinking is called for.

Reflection

If you believe that you have leadership qualities then discover more about your style by asking yourself some of the following questions. Work through each question and note down your answers.

■ Consider your career up to this point in the LIS sector. What are the key strands of change that you think have affected your sector in particular? What leadership roles do you see?

■ Think about a recent example of when you were trying to convince someone, a group, anyone about an idea you had. List the creative and innovative methods you used to enthuse and influence people.

■ If you work as part of a team that are disconnected from an idea, consider how you get buy-in from key staff that could pull the different factions of your team together to realise goals or benefits.

■ How would discuss your service delivery in terms of the global picture, irrespective of whether you manage the service.

■ What opportunities are there for change in the service you are part of?

■ How do you view change? As an opportunity for change and reflection or as just an annoyance?

■ Think about how you could harness unique skills sets, such as people who have worked in other industries or have specific subject knowledge.

■ What is the political agenda in your place of work or sector? How can you influence this?

■ Do you have supporters and sponsors outside the library service? Would people recognise you outside the library?

■ What aspects of entrepreneurial spirit and thinking do you consider would be most useful to your library service? Can you identify any person in the library team who may fit the bill?

(Cont'd)

- How do you feel about ideas that may never have been tested in your library environment, for example customer service from the retail sector, project management from the construction industry and processes from Formula 1 racing?
- Do you understand the difference between having passion and being married to your job?

Can I train to be a leader?

I graduated from library school in the mid-1990s and leadership in the LIS was most definitely not on the curriculum for most LIS courses. This may have changed, but it hardly seems surprising that LIS professionals are now somewhat reluctant to accept the challenges and, as Roberts and Rowley (2008) suggest, 'prefer to focus on library issues'. There is a perception that 'leaders are born', but is this true? Can anyone be a leader and can anyone learn the skills to be a leader? This is a complex question. As already stated, leaders and managers have quite different skills and you do not need to be a manager to be a leader. I think a more important question to ask is: 'Do you want to be a leader?'

Leadership, although highly prized, can seem a scary and risky prospect for most of us. As the leader you must ensure the survival of your team, you often have to lead older and more experienced practitioners and you have to have authority and discipline within your team. It sounds hard work and there is a good chance that most of us may not survive the process.

Although there is a great deal of material written about leadership there is a slight problem: it is a difficult subject to encapsulate and it is a little fuzzy round the edges to define completely. Heye (2006) quite rightly pointed out that leadership 'is hardly tangible'. In library and information work we like to deal in tangibles, we are trained in tangibles.

We answer enquiries, we develop current awareness services, we catalogue books, we create a database. How can you learn the skills or the rules if the subject itself does not seem to be so clear? Ask yourself: 'Can you spot a good leader?', 'Do you know any good leaders?' and 'What are the skills or traits of a good leader?'

Obviously we can all learn from experience, and most of us will have seen or suffered good and bad examples of leadership, but this is a random approach. Heye further suggests that you can learn from the best, but that you have to make your choices carefully.

Reflection

Start looking around for people you admire and trust in the LIS sector. Perhaps you know them through your place of work, or they are well known in your sector, through your professional association or via a committee or group you are involved in. Work out what you most admire in them: is it specific skills or attributes? What sets them apart from others? What do they do that you don't?

Looking beyond the LIS sector

I believe that there is also much to learn from a more outward-looking approach, and yes that means from the non-information and library world. As someone who has worked for ten years prior to librarianship in another industry I don't have a problem with learning from somewhere else. A senior manager (and leader) from the utilities sector encourages his team to learn lessons from different industries. He asks questions such as 'Who is great at customer service?', 'Who is highly successful at transformational change management strategies?' and

'Where are good examples of organisational knowledge management?' They believe that looking inward to your own industry is short-sighted and dangerous. By looking outward at good practice elsewhere he encourages creative thinking. It is my experience that there is a certain amount of navel gazing that goes on in the world of libraries and this causes a number of problems. Firstly, we are stopping innovation entering the industry and secondly, by not pushing it out to meet others, we are missing an opportunity for raising the profile of our profession.

Reflection

Consider some issues or projects in your place of work and start thinking more outwardly about how you could influence the outcome. Start your creative juices flowing by looking for and collecting evidence outside the LIS sector of people, projects or examples that have similar themes. Take the ideas into your workplace and see what the response may be. Consider even writing up your findings for publication. This may also give you an indication of whether your organisation is the right place for your development into leadership.

Leadership – tangible outputs?

So how can you make leadership more tangible? The answer, get results. And how do you get results? As a leader you need to set the vision, direction and objectives for a team or organisation ... the creative process. The earlier chapters in coaching (Chapter 5 'Tips for keeping up with business as usual and managing change' and Chapter 7 'Taking charge using project management as a tool') will help you and your team in this process. On the other hand, to be successful you need respect and trust from your team. To ensure this you need to be open and honest with your team as well as get things done – action and achievement will speak volumes.

Leadership is not about waiting for goals to be set for you. Your job is to work out the agenda in a political situation, create a vision and work very closely with people to achieve the goals. Here are the key assets:

- vision;
- delegation;
- motivation of others;
- decisiveness;
- crisis management;
- expectation management;
- honesty and integrity.

What traits do successful leaders have?

Obviously this can vary from sector to sector but there are general themes. For example, working in the money markets varies considerably from working in a public library. But there are general themes for a successful leader, and they are nothing to do with being born with the right abilities.

- More often than not leaders are not the smartest technically or intellectually.
- They may not always follow the rules or procedures.
- They can be creative and perhaps have unusual solutions to problems.
- They take risks and occasionally make mistakes but are magnanimous in defeat and always know a good idea when they see it.
- They usually have a visible profile and seem to know the right people.

Manager or leader: know your personality type and traits

Leaders and managers are just regular people (honestly) and by working your way through this chapter you are starting to consider what exactly it is about them that makes them different and perhaps even unique. By design or by organic growth, they may have a better understanding of their core skills, attributes and personal characteristics, and these have an impact on their career and performance. You can also get a better handle on your personality by doing one of the personality tests.

One of the most common personality tests is the Myers-Briggs Type Indicator (MBTI), which is based on personal preferences. There are four scales and you choose a single preference from each scale that most suits you.

- **Introvert (I) – Extrovert (E)**

  How do you interact with the world, people and communities and direct your energy?

- **Sensing (S) – Intuiting (I)**

  Do you prefer facts and hard evidence or enjoy the unknown?

- **Thinking (T) – Feeling (F)**

  Do you like logic and analysis or do you prefer to be driven by what is important to you?

- **Judging (J) – Perceiving (P)**

  What drives you? Structure and stability or free flowing without boundaries?

Using this scale you can assess your personality type. There are 16 combinations of personality type. Dority (2006) reports that the classic MBTI scale for the librarian is ISTJ: introvert, sensing, thinking and judging. My scale is EIFP and this suits the way I work and live my life.

In Chapter 3 ('It's all about you') we touched on personality traits, i.e. your behaviour. If you have not actively completed this chapter then do so now. It will give you further enquiry and insight into the traits that you think are part of your personality make-up. Some have suggested that different traits are required to do particular jobs in the LIS sector (2008), but that with the knowledge you can actually learn these traits.

It is quite common to have your personality measured by tools if you are a senior manager, and there are varying degrees of agreement over their relevance or accuracy. However, they do have usefulness as a starting point.

Reflection

Using the Myers-Briggs test where would you place yourself? Ask yourself whether this fits with your career at the moment and any aspirations you may have. Can you identify some gaps in your competencies or attributes? Think of ways to work on your gaps. If you have a team working for you or if you work in a small team, where do they fit in? It may be a useful exercise for all team members to be more aware of their personalities.

Managers and leaders – let's get emotional

A more recent phenomenon has been the study of 'emotional intelligence' or EI. This is how you manage not just your own feelings but also those of other people and it has been suggested that it is this that gives a leader or a manager that something 'extra special'. In fact it can be this intangible that makes the key difference in being a great leader.

At the start of this chapter I talked about the importance of managing people and the importance of this in relation to success. What is the team like? How will you and your team (and their strengths, weaknesses and characters) get along and get results? Remember your team are the main reflection of your success. Another way of harnessing this knowledge is through a 360-degree test and your ability to work and harness people skills is one of the most important assets you can have.

Emotional intelligence is the ability to deal with people effectively and sympathetically. This can be through motivating, influencing, coaching, delegating, dealing with conflict, giving feedback, managing yourself, using time effectively and planning from days to decades.

Behaviours of managers and leaders

There are a few general behaviours that are common to both leaders and managers. I have grouped these together below.

Getting people to follow you

You may have expected charisma to be one of the key features of good management or leadership, but it is only a small part. You need to be able to deliver against the most basic assets. If you are honest, upfront with people and decisive in actions then you will also succeed. Charisma is not a prerequisite. It may be initially appealing to people but if you fail to deliver then people will not be fooled or remain loyal. So, 'talking the talk' is one part but it is your actions that will impress people and create a good impression.

Working your strengths and weakness

Very few people are brilliant at everything, and managers and leaders are no exceptions. But if they are successful then what they do is play to their strengths and delegate their weaknesses. I know a manager who is very creative and motivates his staff well; however, he is not a finisher. But his large team consistently exceed their targets. How? He has surrounded himself with people who all have the technical ability and skills that he does not. So his creative ideas are turned into workable projects and get finished. The team feel part of the whole process and he congratulates the whole team.

Self-belief

Always believe that what you do will be successful. Visualise the steps in completing a successful project and how brilliant you will feel and those around that are affected by what you have done. Then just do it. The more you think like a winner, the more it just becomes the norm. I believe that I am a lucky person, and if I enter a raffle or a prize draw I will have an expectation of winning. Statistically, I may not win any more than others but I always have an anticipation of winning.

Practice or luck?

I have already mentioned this in the book a couple of times. My late father in law used to say 'the harder I work, the luckier I am' – not rocket science but wisdom from a seventy-something year old who had worked all his days as a welder. He realised early on that constantly practising your craft and looking out for opportunities were the keys to success, and for him it was about always being able to provide for his family and hold down a job. So he made sure he always practised his craft and developed his skills with new welding technologies that would make him more employable. Being positive and confident in your abilities, even in a negative atmosphere, works every time. Over time he learned to be lucky and focusing on the positive was the key to success.

Positivity and enthusiasm

I find myself quite irked by the growing cynicism in librarianship. It is a personal preference and I do all that I can to escape from it. I do believe there are problems in our profession and not everything is rosy, but I also believe that concentrating on all that is bad gets us nowhere. I believe that whatever you focus on will be what you get. Living in la-la land – I don't think so! I believe instead in focusing my energies elsewhere and that having a positive outlook leads to a better future, better focus, more clarity, more action, more possibilities, more control and a variety of options. It has been said by some that just being positive and enthusiastic does not mean that everything will work out – this is absolutely correct. But countered with pragmatism and the ability to create vision and clarity and to project manage it is hard to see why enthusiasm and positivity should fail. The more you are enthusiastic, the more you will enthuse others around you. This is not an artificial state of mind, or some 'off-the-shelf' psychobabble, but a real solution to getting things done. It's hard not to feel excited and positive when you are around people who present solutions or ideas in a way that encourages a more positive outlook. I know how I would rather spend my time.

Honesty, trust and availability

Why would someone follow a manager and leader and work hard for them? How do they manage to gain such respect and productivity from people? Firstly, be open and honest about your intentions as a leader or manager. People can spot a mile off if you are feathering your own nest and are really a solo player. Build your ambitiousness into your plans for the team, be ambitious for your team and give them opportunities for growth and success.

Listen carefully to what people are telling you. Be interested in others. It's a social thing really. If you can't do the small talk then people will find it hard to connect to you. If you can't do the 'how was your weekend' chat then you need to start practising. Also, let people have the time to do things their own way. This can be hard and frustrating – have you ever felt that you may be quicker doing it yourself? You must resist, because in the long run trust will give you better outcomes. When everything goes well and there is success then give credit where it is due. Remember your success as a manager or leader is reliant on others.

It is taken for granted that responsibility is part of the job as a manager or leader, so be clear about your responsibilities, but also own up to it when things go wrong.

Hard work

Are you a hard worker? What would your colleagues, team members or co-workers say about you? Can you deliver the goods? Can you roll up your sleeves and get on with it? Do you pitch in to get the job done? Do you expect to pass the work onto subordinates now that you are the manager/leader?

Leadership and management skills – here I come!

Experience

This is a no brainer. Try to use some of the reflective points throughout this chapter to gain experience where you can. For example, if you need experience of management skills then look for opportunities now for learning skills in working with that end in mind: how to get results, making decisions, solving problems, setting and managing budgets and costs, understanding what the numbers say to you, strategic thinking.

- Ask your boss for some direct experience of these areas in your own organisation.
- Look for opportunities outside your direct employment such as committee work in professional associations.
- Voluntary board work in other organisations will build up generic transferable skills.

Peers

Meet up with your peers and exchange ideas about how they have acquired their skills. You may be surprised by the things people get up to!

Role models

Identify good examples of people and best practice. Use colleagues and actively search for evidence in the library sector. Work out what traits these role models have and how they developed their careers.

Shadowing

Find out whether there are any opportunities for you to shadow a manager/leader. What is it about their personality and character that makes them successful or not? Use a journal to record your thoughts and ideas.

Coaching and mentoring

This idea is also covered in Chapter 5 ('Tips for keeping up with business as usual and managing change'). This can be a useful tool if you want to have an outside perspective and are open to ideas from different sectors of the industry or outside the industry altogether. It can also be challenging in that you must be willing to confront difficulties and accept feedback. It is also a process of great responsibility, and you must be willing to put in the time and effort.

Development programmes

Some organisations have developed a route for identifying managers and leaders, sometimes called the 'fast track' or 'pipeline'. While such a route is generally to be found in the larger organisation, you may also find it in areas such as the health sector and academic or public libraries where there may be a leadership programme combining formal instruction and mentoring. If you work in a special library, then find out about accessing the general management and leadership programme.

Formal education

Formal education will always play its part, so look out for training from the professional associations, specialist consultancy groups and postgraduate education such as MBA programmes.

Study people and best practice from other industry sectors

One of the best ways to develop creativity and innovation is to find evidence of good practice from other industry sectors. Follow up the research phase with seeing best practice in action either in the workplace or going to a conference that you would not normally attend.

Projects that test skills

If you are truly serious about acquiring these skills then put your money where your mouth is and look for a project that will test your mettle, especially if it is a pressing issue of business growth or strategy. For example, you could develop a discussion document to circulate outside the library on the the cost-effectiveness of the new document delivery service or the impact of the literature search service on patient care, or you could investigate a hospital's grant funding support or the improvement in literacy rates in a socially excluded area.

Reflection and understanding for the chapter

- Have you been preparing yourself for the next level up?
- Do you understand the difference between leading and managing?
- Can you recognise the behaviours and personality traits of leaders and managers?
- Do you understand how to build up experience and skills in leading and managing?

References

Belbin, M.R. (2003) *Management Teams: Why They Succeed or Fail*, 2nd edn. Oxford: Butterworth-Heinemann.

Bryson, J. (2006) *Managing Information Services: A Transformational Approach*. Aldershot: Ashgate.

Castiglione, J. (2006) 'Organizational learning and transformational leadership in the library environment', *Library Management*, 27(4/5): 289–99.

Covey, S.R. (2004) *The 7 Habits of Highly Effective People*, 15th anniversary edn. London: Simon & Schuster.

Dority, K.G. (2006) *Rethinking Information Work: A Career Guide for Librarians and Other Information Professionals*. Westport, CT: Libraries Unlimited.

Heye, D. (2006) *Characteristics of the Successful Twenty-First Century Information Professional*. Oxford: Chandos.

Roberts, S. and Rowley, J. (2008) *Leadership: The Challenge for the Information Professional*. London: Facet.

Williamson, J.M., Pemberton, A.E. and Lounsbury, J.W. (2008) 'Personality traits of individuals in different specialities of librarianship', *Journal of Documentation*, 64(2): 273–86.

Further reading

Adair, J. (2006) *How to Grow Leaders: The Seven Key Principles of Effective Leadership Development*. London: Kogan Page.

Adair, J. (2007) *Develop Your Leadership Skills*, The Sunday Times Creating Success Series. London: Kogan Page.

Otazo, K. (2006) *The Truth About Being a Leader*. Upper Saddle River, NJ: FT Press.

Owen, J. (2005) *How to Lead*. Harlow: Pearson Prentice Hall Business.

Owen, J. (2006) *How to Manage*. Harlow: Pearson Prentice Hall Business.

Peeling, N. (2008) *Brilliant Manager: What the Best Managers Know, Do and Say*. Harlow: Pearson Prentice Hall.

Stettner, M. (2003) *The New Manager's Handbook: 24 Lessons for Mastering Your New Role*. New York: McGraw-Hill.

Templar, R. (2005) *The Rules of Management: A Definitive Code for Managerial Success*. Harlow: Pearson Prentice Hall Business.

Watkins, M. (2003) *The First 90 Days: Critical Success Strategies for New Leaders at All Levels*. Cambridge, MA: Harvard Business School Press.

11

Going it alone – being an independent information professional

After you have read this chapter you will have a better understanding of:

- what an independent information professional is and what they do;
- good and bad things about being independent;
- whether you need different skills to work independently;
- setting up in business: what about clients, markets, overheads and money?
- adding value to your deliverables;
- how you get and maintain professional development and support;
- strategic planning for the independent business.

Introduction

You will either be excited by the prospect of this chapter or completely terrified. It is my experience that these are the two main emotions that people have when thinking about being an independent (freelance) worker. It is also my own personal experience that I can feel these two emotions on a daily basis.

Imagine this scenario. It's Monday morning and the start of the working week, and you have to brace yourself for the ten-second commute to work. Fortunately you can break this arduous journey by picking up a cup of coffee en route from the kitchen. As you enter the office your family pets have already taken up their usual spots for their daily sleepathon. Your desk is positioned near the window, where you have natural sunlight and a good view of the local sports training club ... It sounds idyllic, but what really are the highs and lows of working for yourself, and is working independently the right career move for you?

What is an independent and what do they do?

Independent information workers basically cover the same broad information categories as other library or information jobs – generally it is about finding, organising, using and managing information in some way. There are probably three broad strands that you can harness for doing independent work:

1. Traditional skills such as cataloguing, research, training can all be used to great effect as an independent.

2. Newer information skills such as knowledge management and managing such assets means that they need people to meta-tag and build taxonomies, research market opportunities and do competitive intelligence.

3. Everyday activities can also get you involved in a library or information service on a consultancy basis such as marketing your service, building websites or training clients in using online databases.

Independents generally work on their own, but occasionally (or sometimes) join forces. Independents very rarely work in isolation. They provide information services such as research, analysis, information management, consulting or training. They charge for their services either by project or on a daily (or hourly) rate. Many independent workers have worked as librarians or within information services before setting out in their own business. Some may have started in other fields and have migrated into providing information services within their sector. For example, I know a microbiologist who is an editor for a biomedical journal and considers himself an information specialist.

Here are some of the work you may consider doing:

- consulting – facilitating and/or implementing change for a client, such as a new service or auditing an existing service;
- research – scoping, researching and delivering a value added resource that supports some part of the organisation's goals;
- training – developing and delivering training sessions for the information profession or professional within an industry sector;
- writing and editing – for journals;
- competitive intelligence;
- indexer and abstractor – for publishers and online databases;
- contract/agency work – cataloguing, updating information resources and covering for staff absences.

This sector offers work in a great variety of fields and you will find that your experience up until now and the areas that interest you will influence what you do. The title of your job may be freelancer, contract worker, researcher or consultant.

Most independents work on their own and are based at home. However, I have also worked for a client and been based in their offices for part of the time. If you are planning a business with more than one person then you may have to consider getting office space. Consider also how you want to work – full time, part time, flexible time, evenings, weekends? Can you accommodate tight deadlines 24/7, or are you looking for work that can fit more easily into your personal commitments? Perhaps you should go back to Chapter 2 ('Your LIS career I presume?') and rethink what type of work interests you and how you want to work as part of your lifestyle.

I started working freelance by accident, a short-term stopgap en route back to the NHS from the private sector. That was eight years ago. I am generally involved in project/research work, some consultancy and writing. I do have a strong specialism in the health and social care sector, but I also have experience of the business sector and the construction industry. This all helps to build up my more generic research and consultancy skills. I work part time and try to take on only what I can actually do that fits in with my private life. I generally work in Scotland, but this is starting to change and recently I have been using my generic skills in consultancy, business planning and research to do work outside health care and in other geographic locations. As your business grows then expect your service to change also.

Managing time as an independent

The great joy of being an independent is the chance to be more in control of your own destiny, managing your own workload and choosing to do things that you find fulfilling. However, the same rule applies as in 'regular jobs'. If you take on a project or work then you must deliver. It is your ability to manage the work and deliver on time and to cost that will ultimately be a reflection of your success. As an independent you are cut free from someone standing over you on a regular basis requesting updates or measuring production. Very often you get a job and then return with the finished product.

In my world, sometimes a research project can last 4–6 months which can seem like an eternity. Perhaps I could just pop into town and meet a friend for coffee. Fancy going for a swim? With the pool across the street it's a temptation. My favourite film is just out on DVD – perhaps just a peep before I start. Laundry piling up for washing and ironing? Or am I just too tired and need another hour in bed? Whatever the reason, you have to resist. This is how you are going to earn your living, pay your bills, put bread on the table, have holidays.

This all may seem a little harsh and I am certainly not going to preach about how you have to live your life. But if you are going to make it as an independent one of the initial key things that you need to get a handle on is the ability to manage your time effectively and efficiently. I find that one of the benefits of being independent is the ability to manage my own workload and have a more balanced lifestyle. I have a partner and two small children, one at school (just) and one at kindergarten, and I work part time. I have one day during the week when I don't work at all, Saturday. My workdays are short, as I have to work round school and after-school activities. I also generally work Sunday afternoons and at least one/two evenings during the week depending on paid projects or the amount of development I need to do. I take regular holidays in line with school semesters and my lightest workload is in the summer period (July to mid-August) as it's the main school holidays. My standard day starts around 9.15 a.m. and finishes at 2:15 p.m. for the school pickups.

I always take a proper lunch-break for 15–20 minutes so I have a properly defined day for work.

I am writing this chapter and it is a Sunday afternoon. If truth be told I would rather be out and about with my family and friends. However, I have more flexibility during the week and if I worked in a regular work environment I would not be able to do as much around my family on weekdays. When work is very busy and deadlines are looming there is more evening work. The key piece of advice is to manage your time accordingly. Take on as much work as you want, but you must be able to manage your time and priorities accordingly. Use the tips and techniques in Chapter 6 ('Making the time for managing your career') and Chapter 7 ('Taking charge using project management as a tool') to help you manage yourself and your goals.

Good and bad things about being independent

One of the sheer joys of working independently is the ability to be flexible in workload volume and type. I don't miss my days being 'mapped out' or being caught up in office politics. I don't take on too much work and plan for 'minimal work periods' such as school holidays.

I work in an industry sector that I am greatly interested in. I feel that I know where my strengths and weaknesses lie and I concentrate on being able to offer 'value-added' products and services.

I really am a people person, which may sound funny when I choose to work alone. However, I get to meet so many interesting people on a regular basis through the variety of projects I get involved in. It allows me to develop a view in depth of organisations and sectors I would never get otherwise. Strange though it sounds, one of my loneliest jobs ever was as an employee of a multinational organisation working in a large office environment.

However, despite all that is great about independent working there is a downside. Some of the skills for survival will be wrapped up in the type of person you are, your character, and some you can learn on the job. Ask yourself some of these questions.

- Do you have a tolerance for risk and uncertainty? If you are a natural worrier then this may not be for you.
- Could you do or want to do all of these jobs – business planning, marketing, client management, administration, providing information services – and be the only one on the coffee rota!
- How would you cope when things are getting tough?
  - Who do you blame for ineffectiveness and poor decision-making?
  - What happens when a good client announces a freeze on their project funding?
- Work taking over?
  - Work can easily dominate and it can be difficult to 'let go'.
  - Physically you are close to work, your office being in your house generally.
  - Unpaid work such as networking, marketing yourself and going to conferences can really add to your hours.
- Clarity and focus?
  - Be clear about what the business is and where it is going.
  - Manage time efficiently.
  - Do not be distracted by non-work items.
  - Always deliver on time.

Running a successful independent business is not just about the day-to-day operational (business-as-usual) things, but being able to strategically develop your business. Later on in the chapter we will come back to how you can manage your strategic development for the business and yourself.

Skills for working independently

I have already mentioned that some of the skills you need for working in this fashion are already part of your character, but you can also learn some of them. As you read through what follows you will realise that some are quite entrepreneurial in nature, perhaps not something we very often see associated with the library and information sector.

Do you recognise some of these skills in yourself?

- Belief in yourself
  - Like all aspects of career development and taking control this will affect the outcome.
  - Independents generally expect (and know from experience) that their efforts impact the outcome.
  - Independents have doubts like anyone else but feel more in control.
- People skills
  - Enjoy working with people.
  - Rapidly assess people types and possible behaviour types.
- Business and financial skills
  - Marketing.
  - Negotiating.
  - Cash flow management.

- Contractual obligations.

- Operational business planning and strategic development: how does your business work and how can you continue to make money?

- Project/time management skills

  - Be efficient and effective with your time

  - Meet deadlines

  - Scope out projects and manage the workloads

  - Juggle multiple projects

  - Independents generally have strong self-discipline

- Good information skills

  - Perhaps a subject expertise or the ability to quickly master new topics (get up to speed quickly).

  - Understand how to package information to meet the needs of your client.

  - Good generic research skills including how to use commercial databases, print and Internet resources and perhaps even telephone interviewing and questionnaire design and analysis.

- Private and public sector experience is useful though not essential.

- Energy and enthusiasm for your chosen specialities and for the services you supply. Do not underestimate this skill.

- Entrepreneurial skills

  - Creative and innovative thinking.

  - Tolerating risk based on evidence and research.

  - Have quite a high comfort level with change and willing to try new things.

One of the key skills that has been highlighted by other independents is the ability to be an entrepreneur. Both Bates (2003) and Dority (2006) have cited entrepreneurship to be a major factor for success in running a successful business.

Small fish in a big pond or bigger fish in a smaller pond?

The world is your oyster and it is up to you to think really hard about what you have to offer and your areas of expertise. If you haven't already completed Chapter 3 ('It's all about you') then do so as this will help you identify your skills and expertise. Some of these questions may help you sort out your target market:

- Clients in the library and information market or outside? For example, will you be looking to do consultancy work for libraries in, say, benchmarking services or change management, will you be offering a research service specifically for the emerging markets sector in macroeconomic data or will you be offering bespoke biomedical literature training courses for health employees?

- Will your product be useful and generic enough to be used across a broad range of industries, e.g. research skills or indexing? For example, you may have experience in digitising collections and creating taxonomies.

- Are you specialised in a particular market such as health or business information?

If you can spread yourself across many markets and use generic skills then there is more potential for clients, but reaching that big broad market may be very costly in terms of marketing. There will be more competition and you may need to come in with lower costs to get work.

I have a niche market in healthcare that I regularly do work in. This is a more focused and smaller market, so it can be easier to build your brand and client list, and marketing costs can be considerably less. However, the main drawback (and it is a big one) is that if the market tightens and suffers a downturn then the client list can dwindle. However, you can stem this tide can by diversifying within the market, by offering a variety of products and by developing some of your work for the generic market.

One vital question is: how do you actually get clients? My first client was by chance and I saw it as an opportunity to try something new. It was a fixed consultancy project to facilitate and deliver a new library service. I also ended up doing some extra work which included training library staff in advanced research techniques, and it was this that led to another library offering me work. This has generally continued and at various points I have re-energised or re-engineered my efforts with the business.

Marketing your business is time-consuming – getting your message out, establishing the brand and increasing visibility. I have used a variety of ideas in the past and below are some of the techniques that have worked for me. My advice is to be open to anything that results from these opportunities.

- *Network.* The trick is to relax, don't do the hard sell, listen carefully and show interest. By mingling you learn a lot about different sectors and can develop ideas for future clients and see gaps in the market.

- *Find mentors.* Do you have a mentor or a friend who can make introductions on your behalf? A client of mine offered to make some introductions to senior library and information colleagues in different sectors. Finding a mentor is like winning the lottery, so make the most of it. Remember, mentors are bound to mention other people

217

you should contact. Read more about mentors in Chapter 5 ('Tips for keeping up with business as usual and managing change').

- *Boost your personal network.* I contacted people I knew already and asked to meet them to discover their services, discuss work I had done previously and bounce some ideas around. Keep this social and short; I generally supplied some cakes or biscuits. Again ask them to recommend other people of interest and ask for introductions. I found most people were flattered to be asked.

- *Go to events.* I identified some local events that had a cross section of information professionals and organisations present, mainly through my professional association and a voluntary library and information group I was a personal member of.

- *Make a script.* Be prepared to talk about yourself and have a short succinct statement about what you do. Some people find it hard to imagine what freelance information professionals do.

- *Write for publication.* I identified publications that would be useful in which to showcase my work and worked to have those articles published.

Setting up in business

Where will you actually work, what equipment do you need to operate as a business and how will you actually work, i.e. what procedures will you have for completing work? Remember also that there are statutory and legal requirements to working as an independent such as being registered with tax authorities and whether you are legally registered as a company or a self-employed person. This will vary according to the country in which you live; for example, setting up and working as an independent in the United States is very different to the United Kingdom. Ignorance will not be tolerated in any country, so contact your local tax office for advice on how to best set up your business.

Most independents tend to work from home, so you will need space in which to work. I have converted a small bedroom into an office. Make sure that you have a proper workstation and a good specification PC and screen. Proper equipment is something that you should always invest in, and remember that you will need to update equipment every couple of years so make sure that some of the money you make covers your overheads like equipment. I know some independents, like me, that have back-up hard drives and an extra screen. A fast broadband Internet connection is also a must, while a separate telephone line and fax machine are also useful.

One thing that is sometimes forgotten is to have processes and procedures for work, yes just the same as in a regular library and information service. For example, how will you produce literature search results? Will you have a template for producing training programmes? The more you can do to not reinvent the wheel will be useful.

Let's talk about money

How much do you charge for your services as an independent? This really is the million-dollar question and is the big variable. There are many factors that will affect this figure, including the following:

- Is your market highly competitive?
- What geographic location are you working in? Big cities always have higher fees.

- Are you working in the public, private or voluntary sector? If you work in the public sector or for a charity then they will not tolerate very high fees. If you work in a major city and are involved in the business or financial sector then very high fees will be the norm.
- Are you basing fees on:
  - what you need to earn to pay for your lifestyle?
  - what the market will bear?
  - an hourly (daily) basis that will take into account overheads such as professional development, equipment and supplies, marketing and profit?

As yet there seems to be no magic formula for calculating the fee so many independents need to take a practical and pragmatic approach to working this out. The first item to consider is your hourly rate and then work from there. Remember that as an independent you have other costs to factor in such as:

- equipment and supplies: hardware, software, office supplies and furniture;
- professional development: books, journal subscriptions, associations, conferences and events;
- tax and insurances: consider what you have to do to keep the taxman happy in your part of the world;
- expenses: travel including car and public transport, taxis and flights, overnight stays;
- profits: will there be any?
- pension, sick pay, holidays?

Research as much of your market as you can and try and find out what others are charging for their services. I recently discovered that some large multinational contractors were billing for research contracts around 25 per cent higher than I was and although their type of work was slightly different to my services it gave me a sense of what that client would tolerate for fees. These other contractors also had higher overheads because they were part of university research departments or national consulting organisations.

It is fair to say that experience is the key. The more experienced you become in your field and the more practice you have in estimating work then the more confident you will be in this area. Experienced independents will always be tracking this and look to make their fees and estimates as competitive and correct as possible.

It is my experience that pricing projects as a whole is a better route. I use tools such as project management (Chapter 7) and time management (Chapter 6) to work out a detailed scope, methodology and programme. This will give you a better feel for what the job actually entails day to day. Presenting and agreeing this with the client allows for everyone to know what and when things should be happening. It is also protection for you. If the client asks for extra work then it is plain for everyone to see what the original project entails. If you have a very fuzzy idea of what the client wants then expect your costs to be fuzzy and the possibility that you may expose yourself to doing unpaid work.

Deliverables

Whatever market you work in and whoever your clients are they are expecting good quality work with a high value. I have not been involved in any projects where the outcome of my work is not in some way tied into that organisation fulfilling its goals or reaching objectives. If you think about it, an organisation only has a certain amount of money so every penny they spend should pay for itself. To achieve success and make your clients use you again I also recommend you provide a value added deliverable. As Mary Ellen Bates (2003) says: 'no added value = no perceived value', and although it's not about the fancy packaging it is about making the value of the work stand out and very usable.

For example, I have been working on an audit and resource package for people who have learning disabilities. At the start of the project there was discussion about what kind of information they required and what they wanted to do with it. To get best value for their money I suggested a shorter audit report, with the resources being electronically available on a dedicated web space. I would provide all the resources (over 30 datasets) in spreadsheet format ready for download into their database and work with their information officer on how best to develop a searchable web space. You can guide your client into getting more for their money – in this instance by showing how the information could be better used and in some cases 're-used' and updated easily. Of course I could have costed to do the website myself, but my expertise does not lie in that field and I have no wish for it to be. That's another thing: know what your limits are and when others are better doing the work.

There are other more basic ways to enhance what you do:

- Format reports to look attractive and familiar. Remember to ask the client what their standards and requirements are.
- Use PDF to seal the report.
- Highlight key information by means, say, of an executive summary or bullet points.
- Provide 'information topography' such as important points, a neatly compacted analysis of a subject, key areas lacking any evidence or further points to consider following on from this report.

Professional development

I love working as an independent and I like working on my own, but there is a real downside to this. I really like being with people and although you can keep up to date on developments by reading, connecting with people physically or electronically is I think the best way to stay on top of your own personal development.

Online forums and discussion groups (some are private and some public) allow you to build connections and share expertise or gather knowledge. I am a member of the Freepint community (*http://www.freepint.com/*) which is a wonderful free gem. I am also a member of the private community SHINe (*http://www.shine.co.uk*) which connects me with other professionals working in the Scottish Health Information Network, a priority for keeping up with developments in my niche market. There are some communities you have to pay for membership – one that I would recommend is the AIIP (Association of Independent Information Professionals).

Strategic planning for the independent worker

So how do you manage 'business as usual' as well as strategic development? To help manage this process in my own independent business I have developed a strategic business audit and planning model to gather information about my business and then use the outcomes for my one-year business plan which then feeds into longer-term business plans for 3–5 years.

It is very important that you plan your business. The reality is that unless you have a private income or have won the lottery then you will need to make money from your business on a regular basis and plan for continued change and future income. It is my experience that using a strategic plan has helped me to be more effective in the operational running of my business. I have less time to work now (as I have a young family) and I need to know that how I am running the business is the most effective way for my circumstances.

These are some of the key areas that you need to consider for your strategic plan:

- *Vision and mission* – do you have a clear idea of why you work and what you offer?
- *Situation audit* – do you have data to understand your business and its finances and how are you managing risk and building value?
- *Objectives* – what are your goals?
- *Programmes* – how do you break down your goals into tasks?
- *Review and evaluation* – do you check on progress and the results?

Vision and mission

Let me be quite open: I don't have a vision or a mission statement. I don't feel the need to go to that length and I don't have any employees so I don't need to explain the path that the business is on. However, I do need to know why I am doing the work I am doing and what I can offer clients. Do you?

How are you doing? The audit

When you work independently you are always looking for new and exciting opportunities for generating work and moving into new areas. How can you plan for change when you are not sure that what you are doing right now is effective? The first step in strategically developing your business is to identify and analyse your business as it stands at the moment – use the information trapped inside your business. We can all be busy but are we busy doing the right things? Your potential for growth may not be what you are concentrating on at the moment.

There are five key areas that I review for my annual business audit – bear in mind that you and your business do not operate in a vacuum:

- existing client base and recent projects;
- operational procedures and protocols;
- pricing structures;
- project price estimates against actual costs;
- critical success measures.

Clients and projects

Use the information about your clients and the projects you have been involved in to provide evidence for moving forward. Consider some of these questions:

- How many clients do you have and have you done repeat work for them?
- How do new clients find you? Word of mouth?
- Are your clients limited by sector?
- Are your clients happy with the service and products they receive? Have you asked them?
- What type of projects do you do – research, consultancy, training, etc.?

- Do you take on long-term projects or quick turnaround?

- Are you a specialist or a generalist, either by industry sector or in the type of work that you do?

- What type of projects do clients generally ask you to do and do you get asked to do a lot of similar work?

- Do you have to turn down work on a regular basis?

- Are you working at full capacity for paid work?

- Have some projects not gone well? With hindsight what were the reasons?

Procedures and protocols

As the saying goes 'time is money', so why waste your precious unpaid time by reinventing the wheel for operational processes? Are there certain features of your work that could be standardised? For example, I generally produce scoping papers for large research projects so I have developed a standard heading template for this. I have also developed a standard heading template for reports too. Look for evidence of how you manage and deliver your work and use this information to make your time more effective.

Finances

This is a very important item to consider and not just because money literally puts bread on the table. The financial killer for the independent is cash flow, and you can be turnover rich and cash flow poor. I know this from experience, and I believe I am not alone. We all need to pay for things on a regular basis such as government insurances and taxes, utility bills, business overheads and even cat food, so waiting for money can be tricky. If like me you do large projects over several months then cash coming through the business can be a problem. Either plan for 'desert cash months' or stage payments with clients for big projects. Consider also doing some very short turnaround work.

Use the information about your clients and map out the money you make from them. Some clients may have poorer returns on time spent on projects and money received. The results may surprise you.

Look at your rates

- Look at your rates in relation to the market and remember that geographic differences do occur.

- What do you charge for products? Do you have different rates for different products?

- Are you estimating work accurately? I realised that I was underestimating the time for writing up some projects after examination of past work.

What is success?

Will you know success when you see it? What are the most important ingredients for the success of your business? Every independent will have different success criteria and you must use this information to measure and guide what you are doing on a yearly basis. Is it about reaching a specific turnover? Is it getting two new clients? Is it getting a book published? Is it being able to drop your children at school and nursery everyday and just pay the bills? Make sure you know what constitutes success for you and your business.

So where are you going? Objectives

Now that you have identified what is driving your business, how it is functioning and the desired state for the future, you can generate a plan with objectives. I generally formulate my business plan to run from April to March because it fits in with the UK financial year and most of my work runs to this time frame.

To build the strategic plan to fuel the next year we need to use the information we have gathered about our business and develop objectives. These objectives will be long, medium and short term, and will be tied into your critical success criteria. It will be the short- and long-term objectives that, once translated, will become programmes and tasks. Having tasks based on your own evidence should result in better outcomes. Be clear and specific about objectives and write them down in terms of the results to be achieved rather than actual tasks. For example, you may want to get two new clients this year (the objective). The individual tasks may include networking, speaking at a conference where you may meet prospective clients or showcasing a recent project in an industry-specific journal.

Implementation, review and evaluate

Implement your plan and off you go. Job done? Well no, not really. Make sure that you review and evaluate what you are doing on a regular basis. Personally I like to review my plan every quarter – it gives me a sense of stability and purpose and keeps me focused. Remember to evaluate your plan and bear in mind that just because you didn't tick something off it does not mean you failed. Perhaps you learned some other valuable lessons.

> ## Reflection and understanding for the chapter
>
> There are some key questions that you must consider if you are starting out working as an independent.
>
> - What is you 'elevator speech'? By that I mean if someone asks you what you do, can you answer in around 50 words and clearly demonstrate the value of what you do?
> - Who and what is or are your competition?
> - How will you get a client as an ongoing business?
> - How will you pay the bills if you have no work for a year?
> - What is your strategy for keeping up to date with developments in your field and your own professional development?
> - What is your business planning strategy for the short, medium and long term?
> - What is your brand?
> - What is your contingency for taking holidays and for illness?
> - Would you consider subcontracting work?
> - How will your project proposals and scoping look like?
>
> Now you have reached the end of this chapter you should understand:
>
> - what an independent information worker is;
> - how to set up in business as an independent;
> - what skills are required as an independent;
> - how to manage yourself as an independent professional.

Further reading

Bates, M.E. (2003) *Building and Running a Successful Research Business: A Guide for the Independent Information Professional.* Medford: NJ: CyberAge Books.

Dority, G.K. (2006) *Rethinking Information Work: A Career Guide for Librarians and Other Information Professionals*. Westport, CT: Libraries Unlimited.

Sabroski, S. (2002) *Super Searchers Make It on Their Own*. Medford, NJ: CyberAge Books.

Part 4

A complete framework for personal strategic planning

Personal strategic planning

I said at the start of this book that we would be on a journey of enquiry regarding our career as a LIS professional. There has been reflection, self-awareness and hopefully self-knowledge along the way. This book was written to help the LIS professional work out the most effective method for incorporating their goals into their personal circumstances and their personality. All the chapters were written to provide more understanding of the different tools and ideas that need to be considered in our efforts to take charge of our careers. In the introduction I told you that this book is environmentally friendly – it can be readily re-used at different points in your career in the information sector. It provides a methodology to come back to, and rethink your career goals and aspirations at whatever point you choose.

There is a lot in this book and each chapter can be read as a stand-alone section. However, the book was designed to be most effective in taking charge of your career if the chapters are used to plan, manage and deliver tangible results. In the same way that an organisation has a strategy for how they are going to implement change and make themselves ready for future development as well as ensure that they are still in business, I think that we as information professionals need to be strategic about our own ongoing development and future profession. I call this 'personal strategic planning'. It is the big picture, 'the whole shebang', everything – all that we as professionals need to take us from 'A to B', depending on what your 'A to B' is.

Here is a recap of the book following its structure in four main parts.

Part 1 The backbone – skip this at your peril

The chapters in this part form the backbone to taking charge of your career as a LIS professional; you will find it costly to skip over them. These chapters help you explore your personal preferences and experiences so far and ask you to identify the questions you have about your career. The reflective practice and introspection that is in these chapters can be quite challenging. However, if you persevere you will find the results more rewarding and rich. If you are finding it very difficult to work in the reflective sections then why not 'chum up' with a colleague and work through them together. If you work in a specific industry sector and are part of an association then why not use one of the chapters as a study day and work in teams. A very good option is to find a mentor, preferably not a colleague or your boss, to help you work through the sections. I would further recommend a mentor or coach from another industry sector; this is especially useful if you are working on your management and leadership skills.

- Chapter 2: Your LIS career I presume?
- Chapter 3: It's all about you
- Chapter 4: Check out the view – the LIS landscape

Part 2 Everyday tools for taking charge of your career

These are the tools for the everyday management of your professional development and career. Do not underestimate the power that they will have and the tangible outcomes they can give. The tools are designed to help you think about how you manage and incorporate change and professional personal development. There are many tips on day-to-day matters and more strategic information on taking charge of your career.

- Chapter 5: Tips for keeping up with business as usual and managing change
- Chapter 6: Making the time for managing your career
- Chapter 7: Taking charge using project management as a tool

Part 3 Different stages of your career

This part covers specific periods in your career. The chapters are designed to be used, and will be more effective, after study of Parts 1 and 2. For example, it would be very difficult to become an independent if you did not understand your skill set, your areas of interest and your ability to project manage and manage time effectively. And as an independent, managing your day-to-day and longer-term professional development is a priority for the survival of your business.

- Chapter 8: Career breaks
- Chapter 9: Starting out, making it count
- Chapter 10: Managing and leading
- Chapter 11: Going it alone – being an independent information professional

Part 4 A complete framework for personal strategic planning

The short chapter in this part brings all the tools and ideas together for taking charge of your career.

- Chapter 12: Personal strategic planning

Final thoughts and tips

Throughout the book seven key aspects to taking charge of your career have been consistently emphasised:

1. Remember that you are taking charge of your career and are in control of yourself. This is a very empowering situation to be in.

2. Take into account your personal circumstances and characteristics.

3. Define what constitutes success for you.

4. Have specific and measurable goals, and write them down. What are the success criteria for you, and what will be the benefits to you as a person and an information professional?

5. There are powerful tools available to help you manage and implement the changes and development you want for yourself. They are invaluable aids for the everyday and for the future.

6. See your progress as a journey, not necessarily a final destination, so don't discount the experiences you will get en route.

7. Forget perfection – there are many routes open for growth and personal satisfaction.

Keep these seven aspects in mind and you have the foundations for taking charge of your career. Work on the reflection and the introspection and you cannot fail to be in charge of your career. A career in the LIS sector is rich in rewards and opportunities, so what are you waiting for?

Good luck on your journey!

Appendix:
Templates for project
management checklists

The four templates on the pages which follow may be used when working through Chapter 7 'Taking charge using project management as a tool'. Each checklist template is based around the life cycle of a project. The templates may be copied and re-used as many times as necessary.

Checklist A.1 Initiate and define the project template

Use this checklist to record basic project details. You may copy and re-use this sheet as many times as necessary.

What must the project achieve?

What are the project objectives?

What is the scope of the project? (Be specific and list who will do the work.)

What is the timescale?

Are there any key dates or milestones?

What resources do you need – people, money, equipment?

Checklist A.2 Record risks and issues template

List your tasks and associated risks/issues. Also consider appropriate actions you could take.

Project details

Task	Risk/issue/constraint	Impact	Action

Checklist A.3 Record tasks and estimate time durations template

Use this checklist to record tasks and time durations. You may copy and re-use this sheet as many times as necessary.

Main task   **Time estimate (hours/days etc.)**

Sub-tasks

Main task

Sub-tasks

Main task

Sub-tasks

Main task

Sub-tasks

(Cont'd)

Main task

Sub-tasks

Main task

Sub-tasks

Main task

Sub-tasks

Checklist A.4 Action plan template

Use this template to work out your action plan. You may copy and re-use this template as many times as necessary.

Task	Responsibility	Start date	End date	Time estimate (hours)	Overall duration
Main task 1					
Sub-tasks					
Main task 2					
Sub-tasks					
Main task 3					

Sub-tasks				
Main task 4				
Sub-tasks				
Main task 5				
Sub-tasks				

Glossary of basic project management terms

Activity This is a task, a job or a process which requires an element of time and a resource such as money or materials.

Bar chart A visual chart (or schedule) where activities and their durations are shown by lines drawn against a timescale.

Critical activity An activity that has zero float, i.e. a task that must start and end on time.

Critical path A sequence of events from start to finish, whereby the overall durations determine the project duration. The late completion of activities will have an impact of the end date or delay the project.

Completion date The calculated date by which a project can finish, following estimating and logical scheduling.

Duration This is the amount of time it takes to complete an activity.

Float The amount of time that a task may be extended or delayed before it becomes critical.

Gantt chart This chart is particular to project management showing tasks against time. Activity durations are shown using horizontal bars and indicate pictorially the critical activities and interdependencies.

Issue This is a threat to a project that is currently under way and requires alternative and mitigating actions.